THE WHITE MAN'S GUIDE TO WHITE MALE WRITERS OF THE WESTERN CANON

THE WHITE MAN'S GUIDE TO WHITE MALE WRITERS OF THE WESTERN CANON

DANA SCHWARTZ

ILLUSTRATED BY
JASON ADAM KATZENSTEIN

HARPER ● PERENNIAL

NEW YORK ● LONDON ● TORONTO ● SYDNEY ● NEW DELHI ● AUCKLAND

HARPER ⬤ PERENNIAL

THE WHITE MAN'S GUIDE TO WHITE MALE WRITERS OF THE WESTERN CANON.
Copyright © 2019 by Dana Schwartz and Jason Adam Katzenstein. All rights reserved. Printed in the United States of America.
No part of this book may be used or reproduced in any manner
whatsoever without written permission except in the case of
brief quotations embodied in critical articles and reviews. For
information, address HarperCollins Publishers, 195 Broadway,
New York, NY 10007.

HarperCollins books may be purchased for educational, business, or sales promotional use. For information, please email the
Special Markets Department at SPsales@harpercollins.com.

FIRST EDITION

Designed by Jen Overstreet

Library of Congress Cataloging-in-Publication Data has been
applied for.

ISBN 978-0-06-286787-2 (pbk.)

19 20 21 22 23 LSC 10 9 8 7 6 5 4 3 2 1

To her, but also to me.

One must shed the bad taste of wanting to agree with many. "Good" is no longer good when one's neighbor mouths it. And how should there be a "common good"! The term contradicts itself: whatever can be common always has little value. In the end it must be as it is and always has been: great things remain for the great, abysses for the profound, nuances and shudders for the refined, and, in brief, all that is rare for the rare.
—FRIEDRICH NIETZSCHE

So it goes.
—KURT VONNEGUT

CONTENTS

INTRODUCTION

Welcome to *The White Man's Guide to White Male Writers of the Western Canon.*

I'm happy you're here. Or at least I would be happy if I didn't maintain an air of disaffected ironic detachment at all times. You've probably seen me sitting on the quad, rolling my own cigarette, loose tobacco spilling into my worn copy of *As She Climbed Across the Table*, by Jonathan Lethem. Yeah, it's pretty beaten up; I've read it a couple of times. It just inspires me, you know? Like, right now I think I need to take out my journal and jot down a quick poem. It's called "Orin Incandenza,"[1] and I usually don't like people to read my unfinished work, but maybe I'd let you take a look if you wanted to come back to my dorm room later tonight?

If you are not yet a white male novelist who has established himself as an essential part of the Western Canon, fear not: this guide is here to help. I will teach you everything you need to know to become the chain-smoking, coffee-drinking, Proust-quoting, award-winning writer you've always known you

---

1. That's a reference to *Infinite Jest*.

should be. And if you don't win awards, it's because those awards are for mainstream sellouts who wouldn't know honest literature if it sidled up next to them with an old-fashioned at the Algonquin.

Not a white man? Not to worry. The White Male Writer isn't a hard-and-fast demographic; it's a state of mind (although you could consider changing your name—the Georges Eliot and Sand did pretty well for themselves).

TIP

If anyone asks if you want to discuss "Bartleby, the Scrivener," by Herman Melville, just smile slyly and say, "I would prefer not to."

I have been afforded the privilege of both an elite liberal arts education and an intellect that has allowed me to comprehend, and therefore unpack for you, the Western Canon in its entirety, and thus, I feel it is my duty to share my wisdom with the less fortunate.[2]

And so, whether you're an established novelist or

---

2. I have also been published in several obscure literary journals that, unlike some of the larger commercial entities, recognize my voice.

grad student, English lit major or literary hobbyist, or if you've ever considered writing a 15,000-word short story about a man riding a train that's really about the decline of the American middle class: this book is for you. Keep it on your person at all times just in case: you never know when your local barista won't know the difference between a drip coffee and an Americano and will need a helpful visual guide.

DRESSING LIKE A WRITER

First things first. If you're going to be a writer, you need to look like one.

Start with the head and work your way down. You're going to need a cap—the slouchier, the better—in order to cover the hair that you're too busy to cut or wash as instead you are thinking great thoughts. The slouchy hat is an essential element of a writer's wardrobe. A hat itself harkens back to an era of typewriters and smoking indoors, but unfortunately any attempt to pull off a fedora in the twenty-first century will leave you looking like either:

A. An amateur magician/pickup artist
B. A seventeen-year-old white boy who owns a katana and is waaaay too into Japan
C. Justin Timberlake

All of the above are equally terrible. Avoid base-ball hats unless you are a knuckle-dragging Neanderthal slowly evolving a beer belly. Flattop caps are acceptable only if you are over seventy years old, or a cast member in a production of *Newsies*.

Spend as much money on your glasses as you can in order to make it look like you spent no money at all. The same should be true of your T-shirts, blazers, jackets, footwear, and jeans. The goal aesthetic is graduate school T.A. who needs the money even though your parents have already given it to you. Remember, you now represent the workingman.

METACULOUSLY UNKEMPT HAIR

LOOK OF EXISTENTIAL ENNUI

THREE DAYS' SCRUFF

IS THIS JACKET IRONIC?

IMPRESSIVELY WORN COPY OF DAVID FOSTER WALLACE BOOK

SMOKING KILLS, BUT SO WHAT?

SNEAKERS

FAMILIARIZING YOURSELF WITH THE CANON

What is the Western Canon? It's the foundation for anyone who hopes to ever call himself "well-read." Familiarization with the Western Canon does not guarantee that you will navigate every dinner party you attend (and there will be many) with grace and aplomb, but without it, you have doomed yourself to failure.

Although the Western Canon in broad terms refers to all of the art, philosophy, and culture of Europe and North America, in this book we will focus only on literature. Again, if you plan on attending any social gatherings at all in the near future, I very much recommend you brush up on your Wittgenstein and fine-tune your opinions on Raphael's early work.

But still, this book is a helpful primer for those of you who slept through your sophomore-year English classes and sleepwalked through your essays on Shakespeare. I am here to teach you as only I, a straight white man, can.

Why only white men in this book? Simple: they're the most important ones. They are the most widely read, the most celebrated, the most influential, and, if I'm going to be blunt, the most talented. I mean, sure, there are some ladies who have had a pretty good go at the whole "writing thing," but how could a woman ever capture *my* experience? And by "my experience," I mean my experience as a white man.

GETTING A WRITER'S EDUCATION

If you want to be a writer, you should attend an Ivy League university, where your roommate happens to be the nephew of a senior editor at Knopf, and you should go on to get a summer internship in New York City. This internship will not be paid, and unfortunately you will have to suffer the indignity of living in an apartment that your parents pay for. But soon, your struggles will pay off, and you will be accepted at one of the nation's most prestigious MFA[3] programs.

If you can't do all of that, I hate to say it, but it sounds like you won't have the commitment and discipline necessary to make it as a writer. I can't do anything about that, but I can attempt to teach you.

---

3. Master of fine arts. I can't spoon-feed everything to you.

WHITE MALE WRITERS

William Shakespeare

(1564–1616)

MOST DRAMATIC

"Some are born great, some achieve greatness, and some have greatness thrust upon them."

You know who William Shakespeare was. If you don't, finish eighth grade and come back.

The Bard was born in Stratford-upon-Avon and is credited with writing thirty-nine plays, 154 sonnets, and two narrative poems during the reigns of Queen Elizabeth I and James I. Pretty impressive for the son of a glove-maker, huh? We'll get to that.

At eighteen years old, Shakespeare married a twenty-six-year-old named Anne Hathaway who never starred in any Academy Award–winning films. By 1592, ten years later, Shakespeare's plays were being performed on the London stage, and here's where the important stuff begins.

So *did* Shakespeare really write all of his own plays? Like I said, it seems surprising that a working-class man without access to an MFA program would be so prolific in so many different genres. Remember, Shakespeare's father was a glove-maker, and so it's not as though he received the type of education that would have been afforded to a child of nobility like, say, Sir Francis Bacon. How could a nobody get so good at writing dramas *and* comedies *and* histories *and* sonnets *and* also have time to figure out the perfect goatee for his face shape?

Shakespeare also seemed to have some difficulty successfully spelling his own name when signing his works, but that I'm apt to dismiss because who among us hasn't adopted several practice signatures and/or jaunty alternate spellings of their own name?

If anyone brings up the question of Shakespeare's identity in conversation, or suggests that maybe Sir Francis Bacon actually wrote Shakespeare's plays, here's a real opportunity to engage in some literary tête-à-tête. Just smile a slight, subtle smile and say, "Yes, I've heard that theory bandied about by some of those who studied early theory but haven't since returned to the text." And when people maybe stop inviting you to parties, that just means more time for you at home with a bottle of muscadet and your ink pen.

IMPRESS PEOPLE WITH AN INSIGNIFICANT PIECE OF TRIVIA

Shakespeare had only one son, who died at age eleven, named Hamnet. One can only assume calling the play *Hamlet* was a typo that went on for so long that Shakespeare was too embarrassed to correct it.

SHAKESPEARE WORKS YOU NEED TO KNOW

Or at least need to know enough about to be able to casually reference in conversation. Obviously, I've read all of his works. (I've actually seen several productions at the Globe Theatre, in England, where I've traveled, several times. [In England, it's spelled "theatre."]) But for those of you who might struggle with the complexity of poetry that was performed for illiterate peasants, here's a simple guide to the basics.

Hamlet [1603]: A thirty-year-old college student mopes around his childhood home after his dad dies, rolling his eyes at his high school girlfriend and snapping at his mom and his stepfather, who happens to be his uncle.

BE A PEDANT!

If you hear anyone ever quote "To thine own self be true!" or "Neither a borrower nor a lender be!" that's a golden opportunity to step in as a White Male Writer! Repeat the following phrase, "Actually, the line you're quoting, from *Hamlet*, Act 1, Scene 3, is spoken by Polonius, one of the play's most foolish characters, and quoting it as if it were brilliant advice offered by Shakespeare himself makes you appear the fool as well."

Macbeth [1623]: A Scottish warrior gets pressured into murdering his king by three random witches and also his wife. Women, am I right?

King Lear [1608]: A king goes mad after dividing his kingdom between two disloyal daughters. Women, am I right?

Much Ado About Nothing [1623]: Two people realize they're in love after a play spent constantly arguing and mocking one another. Take heed: If you want to impress a girl at a party, just insult her. If she's your Beatrice, she'll barb right back and won't think you're an asshole for coming up to a stranger and disgracing her.

Henry V [1599]: The young undisciplined Prince Hal from *Henry IV* is grown up, and he leads an army to fight France in the Battle of Agincourt, where, despite being outnumbered, he wins, because he gives a really, really good speech.

The Taming of the Shrew [1623]: Don't worry; there are definitely ways to deal with women who talk too much. Once she realizes how much she loves you, that girl you have a crush on will stop being mean to you.

Romeo and Juliet [1597]: Unless you are a high school freshman, you do not need to talk or think about *Romeo and Juliet*.

HOW TO ORDER BEER LIKE A WHITE MALE WRITER

During Shakespeare's lifetime, coffee and tea were still yet to be introduced and popularized in Britain. Same with water purification. And thus, drinking beer became not only the healthy choice but, really, the only choice. The same is true today if you happen to live in Brooklyn.

SHAKESBEER

For those of you who still order Bud Lights (shudder), it's time to learn to impress others with your brewing knowledge. Bring it up in conversation, as often as possible, regardless of whether the opposite party seems interested or not. Trust me, they are.

If you're having trouble, just choose phrases off the bingo board.

B	I	N	G	O
"Cask-conditioned"	"Mouthfeel"	"Chocolaty"	"ABV"	"I'm just kind of over IPAs"
"Dry hopping"	"It's not even beer if it's not over 80 IBUs"	"Last year's batch was better"	"According to RateBeer . . ."	"Sour beers"
"That maltiness is really coming through"	"I'd drink"	FREE SPACE "On tap"	"It's this super-small local brewery"	"Actually, beer should be served at room temperature"
"Sessionable"	"Nitro"	"Belgians"	"I prefer East Coast IPAs"	"Budweiser is piss"
"Bell's Two Hearted Ale"	"I'll only drink out of a tulip glass"	"Thick head"	"I'm getting really into home brewing"	"Citrusy"

John Milton

(1608–1674)

GOODY TWO-SHOES

"Better to reign in Hell than serve in Heaven."

Let's talk about John Milton, or, as he's more commonly known, that famous English poet who isn't Shakespeare. He wrote blank-verse poems and political opinions so heated that when the monarchy was restored (after Oliver Cromwell's protectorate), he was actually imprisoned in the Tower of London (he got out). John Milton is like if the mascot of Quaker Oats hated the monarchy and Catholics, and if, instead of oatmeal, that guy was incredibly passionate about Latin and the myth of creation.

When he was thirty-five, Milton married Mary Powell, who was either sixteen or seventeen at the time, depending on your source, but who, for *some* reason, was unhappy living with the schoolteacher and pamphleteer twice her age who could generously be characterized as "strict." Mary returned home to her family for three years, during which time Milton began writing extensively on the morality and legality of divorce, for completely unrelated reasons. Luckily for Milton, Mary returned and bore him three daughters who lived to adulthood. (Mary died in childbirth. Very sad for her.)

When Milton went blind just a few years after his daughters' births, they were there to take his dictation and read to him in Latin and Greek. Quick thing worth mentioning: Milton never actually taught his daughters to *understand* Latin or Greek. Milton was a tremendous advocate for equality of opportunity and education, and he privately taught both of his nephews (who went on to become a clerk and a biographer), but he didn't bother with the girls, who were the ones doing all of his writing and reading for him. For them, it was good enough to be able to read other languages without actually knowing the meaning of what they were reading. I mentioned they were girls, right?

So what if his daughters grew up resenting him and accused him of "tyranny"? Is it "tyranny" to wake people up whenever you can't sleep and force them to read to you for hours in languages they don't understand? What was he supposed to do—send them to school or let them get married? He needed people to read to him!

But enough about the girls. Milton married twice more—his second wife died in childbirth (AGAIN), but he stayed with his third wife until his death at age sixty-five. He didn't actually tell his daughters he was bringing home new wives (they heard about Milton's third wedding from a servant), but he was probably too busy thinking about poetry to worry about silly things like whether his daughters would care about the stranger he brought into their home who "oppressed his children in his lifetime, and cheated them at his death."[1]

That's the sort of stuff you're allowed to do when you're a *genius*.

MILTON WORKS YOU NEED TO KNOW

Paradise Lost [1667]: An epic poem in blank verse over ten thousand lines long, *Paradise Lost* deals with the banishment of Satan from Heaven after a failed uprising against God himself and the banishment of Adam and Eve from Eden after eating an apple they weren't supposed to.

---

1. That little quote is from one of John Milton's nephews. You know, who was educated.

Paradise Regained [1671]: Another epic poem in blank verse, this time about the temptation of Christ. It's about a fifth of the length of *Paradise Lost*, because sequels are hard. No hard feelings, Milton. We've all dealt with the sophomore slump.

BEING A DEVIL'S ADVOCATE

In *Paradise Lost*, Milton played the literal Devil's advocate by writing an epic poem telling the story of Satan. Follow his example by taking any opportunity to be the devil's advocate in your own life.

"Unions are an important tool for ensuring workers have adequate conditions."
"If their jobs were really so bad, they would just quit and freelance full-time out of the apartments their parents bought them."

"You should probably read more books by women."
"Pray tell: if books by women are so good, then why haven't I read any, hm?"

"Mother Teresa was a good person."
"Actually, according to the essay 'The Missionary Position,' by Christopher Hitchens, who famously argued against her canonization, she exploited the poor in order to expand Roman Catholic beliefs."

"Smoking kills."
"So does driving in a car, but I don't see you lecturing everyone who gets into a car. And no one in a car looks half as cool as this, unless he's also smoking."

"It's sometimes hard when men—"
"NOT ALL MEN!"

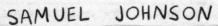

EXPRESSION LIKE HE DOESN'T GIVE A FUCK (SAME)

"JUDGE" HAIR???

Samuel Johnson

(1709–1784)

DEBATE TEAM PRESIDENT

"A fly, sir, may sting a stately horse and make him wince; but one is but an insect, and the other is a horse still."

Samuel Johnson is a writer most famous for a book he didn't actually write. He is the subject of *The Life of Samuel Johnson*, by James Boswell, one of the most important works of biography in the Western Canon, second only to the one that I assume will be written about me as soon as my MFA instructor agrees that the short story I turned in to workshop this week is good enough to submit to *The New Yorker* and things snowball from there.

Johnson himself was a poet, a playwright, and an esteemed literary critic. Though he never really pursued fiction, the highest form of literary artistry (I hardly think one little novella counts), Johnson was still a formidable poet and biographer who celebrated literature and whose works of criticism can be considered art in and of themselves.[1]

JOHNSON WORKS YOU NEED TO KNOW

A Dictionary of the English Language [1755]: Johnson's most important contribution to the literary community was

---

1. Do you hear that, critics? I think you're worthwhile, too!

his *dictionary*. He wrote it single-handedly, in seven years, and it would remain the preeminent English dictionary until the publication of the *Oxford English Dictionary*[2] 150 years later.

Below is a condensed and updated dictionary, which I have taken the liberty to write out for you, with the words you should attempt to pepper into every work of creative writing or speaking out loud you do from now on.

acrimony (/'a-krə-ˌmō-nē/) *n.* Harsh bitterness, particularly of words or feelings.

One of the women—Sandra her name might have been, or Susan—asked to read one of his poems, and when he said no, it was with such acrimony that it surprised even him.

amatorculist (/ăm-ə-tôr'kū-lĭst/) *n.* An insignificant or trifling lover.

He had a series of amatorculists, women (usually blonde, usually young) who gazed up at him with such open generosity of affection that it made him hate them.

---

2. Oxford is a good school, but not as good as the one I attended. It's a private school, in Boston. Well, Cambridge, actually.

aphesis (/'a-fə-səs/) *n.* Loss of an unaccented vowel at the beginning of a word.

"Why don't you come 'round to my place," the brunette at the bar said, eyes and teeth and diamonds glinting. The aphesis in her suggestion made her sound pleasantly congenial, as if they were old friends.

assiduous (/ə-'si-jə-wəs/) *adj.* Showing great care and diligent attention.

"I'm an assiduous collector when it comes to vintage typewriters," he declared, as he welcomed her into his bedroom.

bloviate (/'blō-vē-ˌāt/) *v.* To talk at length, particularly verbosely.

While one of the women in my workshop bloviated on about her story, I contemplated the things I would say while introducing my much better story.

bourgeois (/bu̇rzh-'wä/) *adj.* Of a characteristically middle-class attitude.

My mother asked if I would take her to The Lion King *on Broadway, and it was all I could do not to loudly scoff at her pathetically bourgeois sensibilities.*

diatribe (/'dī-ə-ˌtrīb/) *n.* A forceful, bitter spoken or written argument.

The bar closed at 2 AM, so he was unable to finish his diatribe on people's misinterpretations of Kant's work.

hegemony (/hə-ˈje-mə-nē/) *n.* Dominance, particularly by a nation or social group, over others.

The hegemony of American popular culture means that some adults have lived their entire lives without seeing a single Fellini film.

hirsute (/ˈhər-ˌsōt/) *adj.* Hairy.

I stopped calling her after she forgot to shave her legs before our date—I don't want a hirsute woman.

limerence (/ˈli-mər-əns/) *n.* Obsessive romantic infatuation with another person.

His short story about a man waiting for the subway was so brilliant that the women in his workshop were all struck with limerence.

obfuscate (/'äb-fə-ˌskāt/) *v.* To render obscure, make confusing.

The shadows of twilight crawled from their hiding places, to obfuscate the street in darkness.

paradox (/'per-ə-ˌdäks/) *n.* A seemingly self-contradictory statement.

His loneliness, then, was the result of a paradox: the better you understand the true nature of your fellow man, the more isolated you become from him.

sycophant (/'si-kə-ˌfant/) *n.* A person acting subserviently in order to gain advantage.

Don't just tell me you like my story if you don't. I mean, I know you will, but I want a girlfriend, not a sycophant.

taradiddle (/'ter-ə-ˌdi-dᵊl/) *n.* A petty or trivial lie.

We all knew it was a taradiddle when Marc said he was a Whiting finalist.

vermilion (/vər-'mil-yən/) *adj.* Brilliant red.

She brought her legs up onto the empty subway bench, and I saw her toenails, painted bloody vermilion.

A Journey to the Western Islands of Scotland [1775]: Johnson set out on an eighty-three-day journey through Scotland, particularly the Hebrides, so he could write about Scottish culture and the struggles of the Scottish people. Was Samuel Johnson the first writer to publish a memoir about studying abroad? You decide.

Lives of the Most Eminent English Poets [1779]: An anthology in which Johnson catalogued the most important and influential writers of his era. I am carrying on a similar tradition here. That's what this is. It's a new *Lives of the Most Eminent English Poets*, except better because I'm also talking about people who weren't poets.

JOHANN WOLFGANG VON GOETHE

TOO BUSY
CREATING
TO BRUSH

IRONICALLY
POPPED
COLLAR

Johann Wolfgang von Goethe

(1749–1832)

MOST ANGSTY

"The soul that sees beauty may sometimes walk alone."

It's pronounced "GEH(R)-te."

Repeat after me: *"Guhr. Tuh."*

The trick to the *R* is pretending you have a British accent and barely (just BARELY) curling your tongue back to mark the *R*. It's not a real *R*, but rather a ghostly suggestion of an *R*.

GEH(R)-te.

If you ever hear anyone say "Go-eh-thee," roll your eyes so hard that your eye stems detach from your brain. Let the magnitude of your sneer reverberate for miles, knocking down livestock in its path. You may allow yourself one (1) haughty "Hah!" though it should be less of a word and more of a noise, the sonic representation of your superiority attempting to escape your body.

Goethe achieved international fame at age twenty-five upon the publication of *The Sorrows of Young Werther.* Ever since the eighteenth century, debuts have catapulted writers into celebrity! Goethe was invited to the court of Karl August, Duke of Saxe-Weimar-Eisenach, who made him a nobleman and put him on a variety of councils and in various advisory roles. Although he devoted his life to literature, Goethe also wrote epic and lyric poetry, memoirs, an autobiography, and scientific works on botany, anatomy, and color. Was the science in these writings "correct" or "conventionally accepted by scientists, even at the time"? The answer is no, but when you're young and brilliant and have just been made a nobleman, you get to do whatever you want.

GOETHE WORKS YOU NEED TO KNOW

The Sorrows of Young Werther [1774]: The loosely autobiographical epistolary[1] novel came to embody the Sturm und Drang[2] period in Romantic literature. Werther is a sensitive, brilliant young artist (relatable)

---

1. Dear idiot, it means told through letters. Sincerely, me.
2. *Storm and Stress.* Do you really need me to spell everything out for you?

who falls in love with a beautiful girl named Charlotte, but since all women are snakes who will inevitably betray you and break your heart, Charlotte is engaged to someone else. Overcome with shame and heartbreak, Werther determines to take his own life, and he shoots himself in the head, poorly. He dies twelve hours later and is buried under a linden tree.

If you're ever speaking with anyone who thinks female authors are *so* original and they bring up Jane Austen or Mary Shelley, just remind them that in *Pride and Prejudice*, Mr. Bingley shows up to Longbourn in a *blue jacket* (obviously a Werther reference) and Frankenstein's monster's last word is, also like Werther, "Farewell." *Case closed.*

Faust [1806]: Goethe's most celebrated drama, about the demon Mephistopheles making a bet with God that he can tempt the human Faust away from righteousness. Spoiler alert: Faust sells his soul. If any demons are listening, I will also sell my soul for a bestselling debut novel and an apartment in the East Village.

"Marienbad Elegy" [1823]: In 1821, Goethe spent the summer in the town of Marienbad, where he fell in love with a seventeen-year-old girl named Ulrike von

Levetzow. He asked her to marry him, and the girl declined. It might have had something to do with the fact that Goethe was then seventy-three years old. Goethe, heartbroken, composed what many critics consider his finest work, a poem of devastation and utter heartbreak, which is exactly what one would feel when you're seventy-three years old and a teenager doesn't want to marry you.

WERTHER FEVER

The popularity of *The Sorrows of Young Werther* led to a phenomenon in which young men imitated the character's clothing, and also his habit of shooting himself in the head. In 1775, the novel and Werther-style clothing were banned in Leipzig, and later in both Denmark and Italy.

DRESS LIKE WERTHER FOR HALLOWEEN

What you need:

A bright blue jacket
Yellow breeches
A yellow waistcoat
Riding boots
Angst
A thick German accent

Do not talk to anyone at the party. Instead, just brood and gaze longingly at any woman you see in a couple's costume with someone else.

LORD BYRON

HOT
WRITER
(SAME)

VERY EUSTACE
TILLEY OUTFIT

Lord Byron

(1788–1824)

BIGGEST FLIRT

*"The great object of life is sensation—to feel
that we exist, even though in pain."*

George Gordon Byron, Sixth Baron Byron—poet, critic, general cad—was born a nobleman, and if you weren't, well, there's nothing you can do about that. Even better, though, he was a disgraced noble burdened with huge debts, which is about the most aristocratic thing you can be. He played in the first ever cricket match between Eton and Harrow in 1805 while he was a student at the latter. He went on to study for three years at Trinity College, Cambridge, where he had affairs with men and women. (From Emily Bernhard Jackson: "Byron's sexual orientation has long been a difficult, not to say contentious, topic, and anyone who seeks to discuss it must to some degree speculate, since the evidence is nebulous, contradictory and scanty. It is not so simple to define Byron as homosexual or heterosexual: he seems rather to have been both, and either.")

At Cambridge, Byron established himself as a bon vivant who cared more about adventure and literature than dreary, ordinary things like "money" or "taking care of the illegitimate children you sire." His body consisted entirely of ascots and sneers.

In 1816, Byron spent the summer at Villa Diodati by Lake Geneva in Switzerland, where he was joined by his personal physician, John Polidori; the poet Percy Bysshe Shelley; Shelley's future wife, Mary Godwin; and Mary's stepsister, Claire. Claire had already had an affair with Byron and was tagging along because he was so handsome and talented. (They would have a baby that he didn't deal with as he was very busy creating.)

During a period of incessant rain, the group tried writing scary stories, and Mary Godwin began what would become *Frankenstein*. No doubt she was helped by close proximity to Byron's genius. I wouldn't be surprised if Byron had actually offhandedly said something like, "Hey, what would happen if someone tried to create life? Maybe, like, by animating a corpse? What would that be like?" We'll never know.[1]

FUN FACT

Byron so cherished his Newfoundland dog, Boatswain, that upon the dog's death, Byron commissioned a massive marble memorial at

---

1. Plus, *Frankenstein* is only actually as good as it is because Mary had her husband, Percy, around to do the actual writing for her, I bet.

Newstead Abbey, his ancestral home, which is a completely sane and rational thing to do when you're massively in debt.

Byron also had an affair with the very married Lady Caroline Lamb, who fell so in love with him it was honestly a little sad. Women can be so clingy when you ask them to leave their husband and child to elope with you! It's like, come on, Caroline, get the hint, he wasn't into you. Byron also had a very, *very* close relationship with his half sister, Augusta Leigh, which is all fine and cool because he barely even knew her when he was a kid, and she was very hot. He went on to marry the still-heartbroken Caroline Lamb's cousin Annabella. Annabella would eventually leave him, but only because she didn't understand Byron's tempestuous genius and not for any cousin-affair-related reasons.

Later on, Byron made the brave decision to leave his married twenty-two-year-old mistress (who had left her husband to be with him) (yes, this is a new one) in order to join Greece in the fight for independence from the Ottoman Empire. He grew a sick mustache and posed for portraits like a real hero and everything. Since he was a poet, with all of the military experience of a poet, Byron took command of a part of the rebel army, but before his battalion set sail for the Turkish fortress of Lepanto, he fell ill and died, possibly of sepsis, at age thirty-six. Thank god, because what was he supposed to do if he didn't die? *Get old?* What if he lost his lustrous curls or the rosiness in his lips? What then? Byron died at thirty-six in battle[2] because the alternative was turning thirty-seven, which is basically dying anyway.

BYRON WORKS YOU NEED TO KNOW

"She Walks in Beauty" (1814): This is a poem Byron wrote, drunk, after a party, in order to impress a girl[3] and get her into bed. It almost certainly worked.

Childe[4] Harold's Pilgrimage (1818): A narrative poem about a world-weary and disaffected young man who travels abroad in order to find distractions from his boredom with worldly pleasures. Write what you know, my friends.

---

2. In bed, of sepsis, but in GREECE!
3. She happened to be the wife of his cousin.
4. "Childe," not "child." "Childe" is a medieval word for a candidate for knighthood.

Don Juan [1819]: A satirical poem about the legendary Don Juan, with sixteen cantos and a seventeenth canto left unfinished after Byron's death. In this version of the story, Don Juan is not the seducer, but merely a man constantly being seduced. As Byron knows, it's hard to be irresistible.

HOW TO DEAL WITH STUBBORN EXES

Remember that Caroline Lamb woman we mentioned earlier? Well, she would not get over Byron. And as you have probably dealt with a hundred times in your life (I have), a woman in love with you can be such a hassle. Here are some tips from Big B on how to get them out of your hair.

If she sends you a lock of her pubic hair . . .

Obviously, the love letters you get aren't going to be as well written as the ones you send, but every once in a while you're probably going to receive a very personal effect and a request to return the favor. As Caroline Lamb wrote to Byron: "FROM YOUR WILD ANTELOPE . . . I cut the hair too close and bled much more than you need—"

The correct thing to do in this case is keep the bloody lock of hair on your person, always (as Byron did), as a token of inspiration.

If she requests a lock of your hair . . .

Ugh, what is it with women? All day long, yap yap yap. It's like, "Byron, please stop cheating on me." "Byron, could you please actually stay with me after you ask me to leave my husband for you?" "Byron, hey, this is your friend, it's pretty weird how you're sleeping with your half sister." Ugh. If one of your exes (or one of your fans) writes to you requesting a lock of hair, do what Byron did: send a lock of your *current* lover's hair and pretend it's yours. Oh my god, just imagine the look on her face. EPIC.

If she gives you a nickname in writing . . .

"Mad, bad, and dangerous to know" is about as good of a reputation as a White Male Writer can have. Lean the hell into it.

If she breaks into your house and inscribes a book on your desk with the words "REMEMBER ME!" . . .

Turn it into poetry! Nothing should stir the creative muse so much as someone so obsessed with you that she's willing to break and enter.

Here's the verse Byron wrote in response to Caroline's doing just that:

Remember thee! remember thee!
Till Lethe[5,6] quench life's burning stream
Remorse and shame shall cling to thee,
And haunt thee like a feverish dream!
Remember thee! Aye, doubt it not.
Thy husband too shall think of thee:
By neither shalt thou be forgot,
Thou false to him, thou fiend to me!

If she threatens to "ruin you" . . .

Write a polite letter back saying that you can manage that just fine on your own, and then spend a lot (I mean a lot) of time with your half sister, Augusta, to forget all about what's-her-name.

---

5. The river of forgetfulness in the underworld in Greek mythology. The dead souls were required to drink from it in order to forget their lives on Earth.
6. Virgil wrote (in *The Aeneid*) that souls could only be reincarnated after they drank of the Lethe. I've read *The Aeneid*, in Latin.

CHARLES DICKENS

ASPIRATIONAL BEARD

I'M GONNA DO THIS FOR MUSTACHE MAY

Charles Dickens

(1812–1870)

MOST POPULAR

NICKNAMES: CHARLEY, BOZ, THE D MAN

*"If there were no bad people, there
would be no good lawyers."*

Take a look at that picture, men. *That* is a working-class hero. That is the face of a man who would go on to invent the tradition of ghostly Christmas stories and, eventually, lead to a thousand literary debut novels being described as "Dickensian." My man is an adjective.

Charles had a more or less idyllic childhood up to the age of twelve, when his father was thrown in debtors' prison thanks to his habits of gambling and exorbitant spending. And so Charles was forced to drop out of school and spend ten hours a day working at a factory pasting labels on boot-polish jars.[1]

Dickens eventually graduated from the boot-polish-jar-pasting business and became a journalist, writing satires and covering electoral politics, all eventually amounting to his first writing collection: *Sketches by Boz.*[2]

The success of that collection allowed Dickens to begin writing serialized fiction published episodically

---

1. I had a similar experience when my mother *forced* me to get a job in high school, and I lifeguarded for an entire summer when I was only sixteen.
2. "Boz" was a family nickname, apparently derived from Moses, a character in the novel *The Vicar of Wakefield*, which became Boses, which became Boz.

in periodicals. That's basically the Victorian equivalent of getting into a print literary magazine, you know, like *Tin House* (RIP). Contrary to popular belief,[3] Charles Dickens was not paid by the word; he was paid by the installment, or else, as was the case for *Bleak House* and *Little Dorrit*, his payment was pegged to his sales. And so, next time you hear someone complain that they dislike Dickens because they find him too wordy, rest assured that your companion is not an astute critic but rather a tragic dullard.

SO YOU KNOW

Many of Dickens's works exemplify the "picaresque" novel (from the Spanish *"picaresca,"* from *"pícaro,"* for "rogue" or "rascal"), which depicts stories of loveable lower-class rogues getting by in an unjust society by their wits alone. Another example of a picaresque novel was the manuscript I turned in for my college thesis, about a brilliant twenty-two-year-old third-year who unfairly suffers at the hand of a professor who doesn't understand him and/or is resentful of his many really good ideas.

---

3. Uninformed.

In considering all the White Male Writers I have dutifully catalogued within this compendium, I would be remiss if I failed to mention that Dickens's wild popularity makes him something of a sellout. I mean, the man toured America and was met by hordes of screaming fans, like he was goddam Liszt. A real artist creates not for fans, not to be recognized by an adoring public, but because the work itself is something profound and beautiful. In fact, if your work is *enjoyed* by the *masses*, it indicates to me that your writing lacks complexity and literary merit. Hence why my stories have all been rejected from

The New Yorker, a (sadly) rather mainstream publication in its contemporary iteration.

But back to Boz and his biography: In 1856, when Dickens was forty-four years old, he wrote a play called *The Frozen Deep* with his protégé Wilkie Collins[4] and immediately fell in love with one of the play's actresses, Ellen Ternan. It seems silly to even mention that Ellen (called Nelly) was eighteen years old, and that Dickens, who was forty-five at the time, left his wife of over twenty years to be with her. His wife, Catherine, fled with one of their children (the others would be raised by Catherine's sister), and Dickens never saw his legal wife ever again.

TIP

If you and your teenage mistress are traveling by train with your teenage mistress's mother, and the train happens to be involved in a derailment at Staplehurst in which every car but the first-class (yours) tumbles over a bridge, killing ten people and injuring forty, try to help at the scene as much as possible, but be sure to

---

4. Of course you know Wilkie Collins from his tragically bourgeois detective novel *The Moonstone*.

leave before the police inquest. Traveling with your teenage mistress could cause a scandal.

Some may point out that most of Dickens's female characters are two-dimensional (if not flat-out evil), or that leaving his wife for a teenager is a bit unseemly, and to that I say: sure, but Dickens had a *reason* for being sexist. You see, after his father was released from debtors' prison, Dickens's mother thought young Charles should remain in the workforce instead of going back to school. "I never afterwards forgot, I never shall forget, I never can forget, that my mother was warm for my being sent back," Dickens wrote, and so hating all women on principle therefore seems fairly reasonable.

DICKENS WORKS YOU NEED TO KNOW

Martin Chuzzlewit [1844]: Even though this novel—about a clever young man and his greedy extended family—is one of Dickens's least popular, the author told a friend while writing it that he thought it was his best work. Which just goes to show that the rejection letter I got from *The New Yorker* is completely meaningless. The public doesn't know real literature.

David Copperfield [1850]: A definitely not autobiographical novel about a young boy growing up poor and transforming from impoverished urchin to mightily successful author. His initials are DC, not CD. And traditionally, autobiographical novels are written by women. Men conjure new characters.

Bleak House [1853]: A satire about the twisted British legal system featuring a lovely, perfect, sweet illegitimate girl named Esther and a beautiful, frigid woman named Lady Dedlock (the two types of women).

Great Expectations [1861]: A young boy comes into a fortune, no thanks to this evil hag in her wedding dress and her beautiful, evil daughter. The ending of this book was altered to be (sigh) more palatable to the masses. Instead of Estella marrying the wrong man and growing old and unhappy, the novel ends with her and Pip leaving the charred remains of her childhood home hand in hand. A happy ending is hack.

ANOTHER TIP

Charles Dickens died before finishing his murder-mystery novel, *Edwin Drood*, and without revealing to anyone how the book would actually end, i.e., the who-done-it of the who-dunnit. So, if you think death is imminent, quickly write the first half of a mystery novel just to ensure that you will be remembered for your enigmatic power moves.

HENRY DAVID THOREAU

HOW? RESPECT, BUT HOW?

Henry David Thoreau

[1817–1862]

BIGGEST HIPPIE

"Things do not change; we change."

Who is Henry David Thoreau? Henry David Thoreau is the sigh of a tree as wind moves through her supple branches. He is a hidden and bubbling creek. He is a Man, and an Animal. He is *not* the miserable little creek behind your local mall that's had a plastic bag trapped in it since 2003.

Born in 1817, Thoreau knew from a young age that he would forge his own path in the world, and so, like his grandfather before him, he went to Harvard. But, like a true rebel, when Harvard required a five-dollar fee in order to procure a physical diploma, Thoreau declined to pay. "Let every sheep keep its own skin," he retorted, a pithy comeback *before Twitter was even invented*.

But Thoreau would, of course, not be satisfied by the mundane lives prescribed to his classmates, lives of getting married and "making a living by having a job."[1]

No, rather than become just another cog in the system, Thoreau lived at his friend and mentor Ralph

---

1. He briefly taught at a Concord public school before quitting, so he basically did Teach For America, which is noble but, of course, impermanent.

Waldo Emerson's[2] house, eventually setting out on what would become his most famous experiment and the foundation for his most essential piece of writing: *Walden*. Thoreau would live for two years, two months, and two days at Walden Pond, in a cabin he would build himself, living entirely off the land. That land, for the record, was also owned by Emerson.[3] It was also only a mile and a half from Thoreau's childhood home, but he definitely did *not* go home for laundry or help or anything.

WAS THOREAU A TRUST FUND BABY?

The term "trust fund baby" gets thrown around a lot today, and I feel I must take this opportunity to set the record straight: if, like Thoreau, you *happen* to have the family money or connections that mean you don't have to have a pencil-pushing nine-to-five, you should not feel *guilty*. No, far from it! What you have is an opportunity to *gift* the world with your

---

2. Ever heard of him?
3. Sometimes, when I don't bring a story in for workshop because I didn't feel sufficiently inspired, I quote Emerson: "People do not deserve good writing, they are so pleased with bad."

literature. People should be thanking you for creating in spite of going up against what I would argue is the most challenging circumstance: for truly, what is more difficult to overcome than the singing-siren void of a lack of purpose? Those poor people don't know how lucky they are to have the structure and rigorous discipline of a workday given to them automatically. Besides, they already have built-in hardships to write about. They have it easy.

During the Walden years, a local tax collector found Thoreau and had the *gall* to request he pay six years of delinquent back taxes, this all despite the fact Thoreau was in no way benefiting from government-provided services, infrastructure, or anything of the like, and was in fact CONTRIBUTING art for *free*. When Thoreau refused—on the principle of opposing the Mexican-American War and slavery (and rightly so)—he was forced to spend one full night in jail before someone in his family bailed him out by paying the required taxes (AGAINST HIS WILL!!!—Thoreau would have stayed in jail longer, and wanted to, I'm sure). From that experience, Thoreau wrote an essay, "Civil Disobedience," in which he argued that citizens have a duty to resist their governments when the state performs acts of injustice. That essay would go on to influence Gandhi and the Reverend Martin Luther King Jr. So, when you think about it, the civil rights movement really has Henry David Thoreau to thank.

THOREAU WORKS YOU NEED TO KNOW

Walden [1854]: In his transcendentalist masterpiece, Thoreau recounts the years he spent living at Walden Pond, relying on himself and nothing else in order to survive. He reflects on nature, animals, moral philosophy, and, most importantly, all the importance of reading classical literature in the original Greek or Latin.

HOW TO START A FIRE

If you decide that you, too, plan to sojourn at your family's cabin with nothing but your wits to protect you, it's essential that you know the fundamentals of survival.

First, dig a small pit in the ground and encircle it with small stones, each the size of a woman's breast. At the bottom, crumple some dry newspaper, perhaps the *New York Times Book Review* that yet again sees fit to publish the same old hacks and society sycophants (see page 24) instead of even bothering to read your daring treatises on the American literary community.

Gather a bundle of small, dry sticks, which will serve as your kindling, and bunch them into a cold and brittle bouquet. Place two of the logs you have chopped yourself (of course you chop your own firewood, do you not?) on either side of the kindling, and then stack two more logs atop the first two but in the opposite direction, to make a log-cabin-style square. Continue stacking logs, alternating direction and ensuring there's adequate space between each layer for airflow. Use the matches that you got at that dive bar that smelled like mold and cigar smoke, and light the

kindling. Flint and steel will also work, which will be a good backup if your matches got wet from the flask you had kept in your pocket that night, in case you ended up at an establishment that served only cheap imported beer.

Watch the flames. See how they flicker, diving in and out of life, unencumbered by weight or regret. Fire illuminates, but what does it hide? We are animals here, asking questions of nature to which nature herself is indifferent.

LEO TOLSTOY

LOOKS
IMPORTANT.

BECAUSE
HE IS.

Leo Tolstoy

(1828–1910)

BEST BEARD

"It's hard to love a woman and do anything."

Let's begin here by saying if you haven't read Tolstoy in the original Russian, there's not much I can do for you. Sure, the translations are interesting, but they fail to capture the true breadth of Tolstoy's genius.

Born into an aristocratic family, Tolstoy dropped out of Kazan University in the middle of his degree and began his writing career while simultaneously living a life of gambling, drinking heavily, and engaging in the general debauchery of a young, wealthy person without any responsibilities. But running up gambling debts meant young Tolstoy had to do *something,* and that something, in this case, was to follow his older brother to the Caucasus and join the army to fight in the Crimean War.

But Tolstoy's eyes were really opened when he ~~took a gap year~~ traveled abroad, read Victor Hugo, saw an execution in Paris, and all in all witnessed the gritty human truths that only reveal themselves to white twenty-something boys who come from insane wealth when they go to Europe for the first time.

Returning from Western Europe at thirty-four, Tolstoy married the eighteen-year-old Sonya, who permitted his genius to flourish by working as his secretary, accountant, and personal scribe. On their wedding night, Tolstoy presented Sonya with a detailed account of his sexual history (including the part where he fathered a child by one of his family's serfs. What happened to that serf or to his child? Utterly irrelevant). Truth is the foundation of any good relationship, after all, and we can only assume the teenage Sonya was elated by Tolstoy's benevolence.

In addition to bearing him thirteen children, Sonya was privileged to copy the 1,225-page *War and Peace* by hand eight times while Tolstoy was editing it, because Tolstoy needed clean drafts to send along to the publisher. She also helped him work on the less famous but equally essential book *Resurrection* about the many women he cheated on her with. In the final weeks of his life, the increasingly radical Tolstoy left his wife without telling her, refused to see her when she tracked him down, and then died in a train station.

But at least Sonya was comforted by the fact that Tolstoy also made sure that they never had any money. At this point he had already freed his serfs, renounced his title, and given away most of his wealth to the poor. Instead of his wife and kids, he left the entirety of his estate and future royalties to the fringe Doukhobor spiritual movement. Tolstoy was selected for the first Nobel Prize in Literature in 1901, but he turned it down because he knew the prize money would just complicate things in his life. What could a man with a wife and about a dozen children possibly need money for?

Personally, I've been living as a gluten-free vegan for the last six months (I've found it really helps me connect with my own thoughts on a deeper level), but it's still cute how Tolstoy preached vegetarianism. "A man can live and be healthy without killing animals for food; therefore, if he eats meat, he participates in taking animal life merely for the sake of his appetite. And to act so is immoral." I just wish he were around now to try almond milk, or its close cousin, oat milk.

TOLSTOY WORKS YOU NEED TO KNOW

War and Peace [1867]: The intricacies of nineteenth-century Russian society are laid out through a sweeping historical tale of love, betrayal, family, and revenge, set against the backdrop of the Napoleonic Wars. It's kind of similar to this manuscript I wrote my sophomore year about two roommates living in Bushwick discovering who they are over the course of a year.

The Death of Ivan Ilyich [1886]: A masterpiece novella, it centers around the government official Ivan Ilyich as he becomes more introspective and waxes philosophical on the meaning of life as he dies slowly from injuries sustained from falling while hanging curtains. If you do not know what to do at the end of your novella, always just have the main character die.

Anna Karenina [1877]: A Russian aristocrat scandalizes society when she has an affair with the charming Count Vronsky. Spoiler alert: she kills herself by jumping in front of a train. Women.

HENRY JAMES

EYE BAGS—
GENIUS
NEVER SLEEPS.

LOOKS SERIOUS.
WRITING IS
SERIOUS.

Henry James

[1843–1916]

MOST LIKELY TO STAY
SINGLE FOREVER

"Deep experience is never peaceful."

I actually studied abroad in England,[1] and so I have a special place in my heart for Henry James, the American-born writer who moved overseas and became a naturalized British subject before his death. His works, which bridge traditionalist and modernist literary movements, play with the contrast between repressed aristocratic Europeans and liberal, outspoken Americans. That's one of those little things you pick up on when you study abroad in England, like I did.

James's brother is actually the philosopher William James. Tragic William just got none of the creative literary genes, not unlike my own older brother, who "runs an environmental nonprofit organization" and "is married with three kids." Poor sap will never know creative fulfillment.

Though James traveled extensively and enjoyed friendship with a wide coterie, including Zola, Daudet, and Goncourt, he never married. A lifelong bachelor, James never wanted to settle down, to be tied to a single woman who couldn't possibly understand his emotional range and depth. Bear that in mind next time a girl asks, "What are we?" *What are we?* We are

---

1. Oxford, actually.

nothing but decaying flesh, attaching momentarily and aimlessly until our hearts cease to beat. That, and I'm also sleeping with your roommate.

JAMES WORKS YOU NEED TO KNOW

Daisy Miller [1879]: A beautiful young American named Daisy Miller travels to Europe and flirts with men until it literally kills her.

The Portrait of a Lady [1881]: A beautiful young American named Isabel Archer travels to Europe to learn that any member of the opposite sex who expresses interest in you is a Machiavellian sociopath and marriage is death. It's *dull* and predictable, and I can't imagine anything *less* conducive to the artistic spirit, unless, of course, you find one of those women who is just willing to copy out your manuscripts by hand a bunch of times in a row.

The Turn of the Screw [1898]: A governess cares for two children in a haunted mansion, but the real monster, if you look closely, is sexual repression.

The Ambassadors [1903]: A widower from Woollett, Massachusetts, goes on a mission to Paris as a favor for the woman he's courting: to rescue her son from his decadent European ways. Our hero, Lewis Lambert Strether, becomes alternately enchanted and disgusted with Paris and with the women he's encountered along his journey. Nothing is more interesting than a sad, lonely American man in Paris with multiple women begging to love him.

James Joyce

(1882–1941)

CUTEST COUPLE (WITH
NORA BARNACLE)

---

*"Think you're escaping and run into yourself.
Longest way round is the shortest way home."*

Although James Joyce centered his most famous works in Dublin, he only lived there until he was about twenty years old. After that, he did what every young writer should do at some point: moved away from his family and lived abroad on the Continent until he got famous.

As a child, Joyce studied at a Jesuit school, eventually attending the then newly established University

College Dublin to study English, French, and Italian. Though Joyce's family was Catholic, Joyce formally denied the Church and God at age sixteen, about when I did, when I read my first book by Richard Dawkins.[1] Even as a teen he was a rebel who stuck it to the establishment.

When he graduated from college, he went to Paris to study medicine but quickly dropped out, *not* because lectures in French were too hard but because of a *totally different reason*. Instead, when the death of his mother brought him back to Ireland, he made a living reviewing books, and by singing tenor.

Perhaps the most important day in Joyce's life is June 16, 1904: now celebrated as Bloomsday in Ireland, it's the date on which his novel *Ulysses* takes place. But more importantly, it was the day of his first date with his future wife, Nora Barnacle; on this day she gave him a hand job so good he decided its anniversary should be commemorated in literature forever.

Joyce lived for ten years in Trieste (of course he also spoke fluent Italian, doesn't everybody?) with Nora, who gave birth to their first child. Struggling to

---

1. "Religion is the opium of the people"—Karl Marx. Those of us able to think freely and for ourselves recognize the value in the scientific method.

make any actual money as a writer, he supplemented his meager teacher's income with a little help from his brother.

All the while, Joyce attempted to publish *Dubliners*, his book of short stories, which was met with a grand total of eighteen rejections over the course of eight years, until it was finally published in 1914.

Eventually, his friend Ezra Pound was able to take time out from hating Jews to help Joyce get his novel *A Portrait of the Artist as a Young Man* serialized in the American literary magazine *The Egoist* from 1914 to 1915, igniting Joyce's career as a preeminent modernist in the literary community, which rewarded Joyce with all of the money you imagine comes with being a literary modernist.

JOYCE WORKS YOU NEED TO KNOW

"The Dead" (1914): Don't sell out and marry a girl from Galway.

***Ulysses* (1922):** It's *The Odyssey*, if instead of being about a war hero trying to traverse strange and mythical lands in order to return to his loyal wife, it was about something much more interesting: a Jewish guy walking around Dublin.

Finnegans Wake (1939): A stream-of-consciousness experimental novel about a man who returns to life after
dying from a fall off a ladder, *Finnegans Wake* uses
non-English and made-up language, which makes it
hard for some people to understand, but those of us
who can interpret its lines recognize its genius.

HOW TO WRITE A LOVE LETTER

If you have ever been tempted to slide into the DMs
of that girl in your comparative lit class, take comfort
in the fact that your literary idols did more or less
the same, and far dirtier. Please enjoy the following
excerpts from Joyce's letters to his wife, Nora Barnacle, and be inspired to do better the next time you're
tempted to text "u up?" at 2 AM. And by "do better,"
I mean do dirtier. These are the words of one of the
world's greatest poetic minds, and any girl would be
thrilled to receive one of his messages verbatim. Who
even needs a preface? Just change the names as often
as you please, send away, and watch the girls swoon
at your feet.

BEAUTIFUL WILD FLOWER OF THE HEDGES . . .
   Nora, my faithful darling, my sweet-eyed black-
guard schoolgirl, be my whore, my mistress, as much
as you like (my little frigging mistress! my little f*cking

whore!) you are always my beautiful wild flower of the hedges, my dark-blue rain-drenched flower.

A SUDDEN IMMODEST NOISE . . .

The smallest things give me a great cockstand—a whorish movement of your mouth, a little brown stain on the seat of your white drawers, a sudden dirty word spluttered out by your wet lips, a sudden immodest noise made by your behind and then a bad smell slowly curling up out of your backside.

NO END OF HER FARTS . . .

I hope Nora will let off no end of her farts in my face so that I may know their smell also.

DARLING . . .

Darling, do not be offended at what I wrote.

FRANZ KAFKA

AUTEUR HAIR

HAUNTED EYES

AIR OF MYSTERY

Franz Kafka

[1883–1924]

QUIETEST

"Every revolution evaporates and leaves behind only the slime of a new bureaucracy."

You know you've made it when you have an adjective named for you. "Kafkaesque" means something is surreal and chillingly bureaucratic, as in the world of the author's novels and short stories. But it also means "I am smart enough to know who Franz Kafka is." "Kafkaesque" is a word you should use freely and often in order to communicate that you do, in fact, know Kafka and are familiar with his work.

For Kafka, that chilling bureaucracy had a face: his father's. Kafka was terrified by his overbearing and boisterous father for his entire life, as described in a letter he wrote to his father as an adult.

> Dearest Father,
>
> You asked me recently why I maintain that I am afraid of you. As usual, I was unable to think of any answer to your question, partly for the very reason that I am afraid of you, and partly because an explanation of the grounds for this fear would mean going into far more details than I could even approximately keep in mind while talking. And if I now try to give you an answer in writing, it will still be very incomplete . . .

Kafka gave the 103-page letter to his mother so she could pass it along to his father, but she didn't. The meek woman held on to the letter for a brief period, before returning it to her son.

In Kafka's fiction, the monster isn't just a father, though: it's an illogical and pointless government, endless red tape, punishments from the universe that have no meaning whatsoever, and, above all, the terrible knowledge that you deserve every bad thing that happens to you.

Born to a German-speaking Jewish family in Prague, Kafka lived with his family until he was thirty-one years old, worked in largely boring office jobs, and, though he was engaged to many women, never actually got married. Instead, he frequented brothels and indulged in pornography. According to his friend Max Brod, Kafka was tortured by sexual desire but crippled by fear of underperformance.

Kafka died of tuberculosis in obscurity, and he asked Brod to burn all of his work. Seeing as Kafka was dead and couldn't do anything about it, Brod politely ignored his friend's wishes and instead published all of it.

KAFKA WORKS YOU NEED TO KNOW

Metamorphosis [1915]: A man named Gregor Samsa wakes up to find that, for no reason whatsoever, he has been transformed into a giant insect. He mostly worries about the fact that he's going to have to miss work. His family briefly tries to deal with the fact

that their son and brother has become an insect, but they're all pretty disgusted with him and think life would be easier without the burden of having him around, even when just confined to his room. Gregor agrees and dies.

The Trial [1925]: Josef K. is arrested and prosecuted for a crime by an impenetrable government. Neither he, nor we, know what his crime is, but Josef K. is certain he deserves what he gets, which is being stabbed.

The Castle [1926]: A land surveyor named K. arrives in a remote village, and he's supposed to gain access to a castle and a man named Klamm, but he can't, thanks to bureaucracy.

F. Scott Fitzgerald

(1896–1940)

PROM KING

"Show me a hero, and I'll write you a tragedy."

F. Scott Fitzgerald[1] was born in Minnesota and died in Los Angeles, which is just about the most American way you can do things. One of the greatest American writers of the twentieth century, he embodied the "Lost Generation" of the 1920s—drinking heavily, writing novels and for magazines, marrying a woman you can't save, and having your work woefully misinterpreted by high school students.

Scott was a Princeton man (but I won't hold that against him), and he met Zelda Sayre when his military unit was stationed in Alabama. Everything I could say here about Zelda Sayre was said better[2] by Ernest Hemingway, so I'll let Papa take it away:

> A woman ruined Scott [Fitzgerald]. It wasn't just Scott ruining himself. But why couldn't he have told her to go to hell? Because she was sick. It's being sick makes them act so bloody awful usually and it's because they're sick you can't treat them as you should . . . Anyway let's leave the subject. If you leave a woman, though, you prob-

---

1. Just "Scott" to his friends. I call him Scott.
2. Well, not *better*, just first.

ably ought to shoot her. It would save enough trouble in the end even if they hanged you.

Before I let the subject go, I have to mention that Zelda also had the *gall* to write a fictionalized account of her life with Scott even though she *knew full well* that Scott used their lives for his fiction. How was he going to write about her experiences if she wrote about them first? It just boggles the mind.

Poor Scott spent most of his adult life trying to pay for Zelda's stay in a sanitorium by working a menial, soul-crushing job as a writer in Los Angeles and only having one or two serious affairs. Although his writing was underappreciated in its time, *The Great Gatsby* went on to become one of the front-runners for the title of Great American Novel, misread by high schoolers all across the country who wouldn't know the first thing about unfulfilled longing if it tap-danced across their desks.

FITZGERALD WORKS YOU NEED TO KNOW

This Side of Paradise [1920]: A Princeton man named Amory Blaine (NOT SCOTT FITZGERALD) writes poetry and falls in and out of love with women. He serves in the army and fights in World War I and returns, only to fall in love with a New York socialite who won't marry him because he is Poor.

The Beautiful and Damned [1922]: Anthony Patch (different from Amory Blaine!) serves briefly during World War I and courts a socialite. They are selfish and gorgeous and destroy each other, but only because America destroyed them first.

The Great Gatsby [1925]: Nick Carraway narrates a novel about his friendship with the enigmatic Jay Gatsby, who throws lavish parties and buys beautiful shirts, all with the hope of winning his love, the married Daisy Buchanan. Gatsby ends up facedown in a pool. The American Dream is dead, and you killed it, old sport.

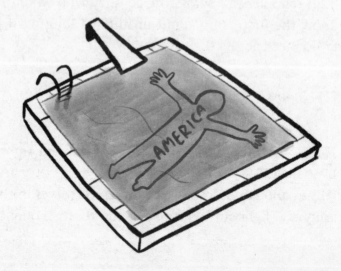

Tender Is the Night [1934]: A young psychiatrist descends into alcoholism and falls in love with one of his patients, an heiress who's had a mental breakdown. The psychiatrist pines for another woman, a Hollywood actress. His marriage is a sham, and so was the American Dream.

The Pat Hobby Stories [1940–1941]: Fitzgerald wrote a series of seventeen stories about Pat Hobby, a down-and-out screenwriter in Hollywood who drinks too much and has run out of ideas. Hollywood will humiliate a man, but not as much as women will.

TIP

Whenever you hear of a wedding that's *Gatsby*-themed (by which they really mean Roaring '20s–themed), scoff and say, "Actually, the *point* of *The Great Gatsby* was to point out the shallow, meaningless indulgence of the Jazz Age. There's no love story there except greed. But all the best to you and your betrothed!" Your friend will be so impressed that he'll probably make you the best man.

HOW TO MAKE A GIN RICKEY

Scott's drink of choice for Jazz Age festivities was a good old-fashioned gin rickey. Here's the recipe for when you go to a party where the host isn't as literary as you are and so you're forced to prepare one for yourself.

What you need

1.5 oz gin

1 lime, juiced

½ tsp. sugar

seltzer water

Fill a highball glass three-fourths of the way full with crushed ice.

Add to the glass 1.5 ounces of gin, the juice of one lime, and half a teaspoon of sugar. Stir while contemplating the contradictions of an America that values the appearance of excess with no concern for whether that excess masks a deeper, fundamental crack.

Fill the glass the rest of the way with seltzer water.

Garnish with a lime and a sigh.

WILLIAM FAULKNER

I FAULK WITH THIS LOOK!

William Faulkner

(1897–1962)

LEAST SENTIMENTAL

"In writing, you must kill all your darlings."[1]

---

1. Such a tragically overused quote, mostly by people who have no idea that it came from William Faulkner. Did you

The South is home to one of America's most beloved literary traditions, the fertile ground from which Harper Lee, Flannery O'Connor, and—most importantly—William Faulkner emerged. But what is the South? More importantly, where is the South? The answer is: nobody knows. The South is not a place; the South is an idea. Even if you, like me, were raised in the bleary train-rail suburbs of Long Island, all it takes to become a Southern Writer is a very promising rejection letter from the *Georgia Review.*

But let's get back to the question of "what."

The South is a decrepit mansion that once held a noble family and now just houses an adult son who has already gambled away half of his inheritance and drunk away the other half. The South is a preacher ranting, spittle and vitriol spewing from his lips. The

---

know? Did you know that it came from William Faulkner? It did. And it doesn't mean you're supposed to kill your darling characters; it means sometimes editing requires you to shave bits of your beautiful prose for the sake of the narrative whole. I had the gorgeous word "lackadaisical" in this book four times before my narrow-minded editor took a hacksaw to it. But alas, William, we are brothers in arms!

church has no air-conditioning. The heat, and society, is oppressive. The South is also dirt, and the specter of racism. If you have, as a white man, for one moment in your entire life occupied your head with the thought that racism was bad, then you are already a writer from the South. Welcome.

Two-time Pulitzer Prize and one-time Nobel Prize winner William Faulkner is perhaps best known for his novels and short stories set in the fictional Yoknapatawpha County, in Mississippi. Faulkner only attended a few semesters of undergrad at the University of Mississippi (Ole Miss to us in the know) before dropping out, writing poetry, and eventually working at the University of Mississippi powerhouse to make ends meet.

SO YOU KNOW

William Faulkner's surname was originally spelled "Falkner," and he changed it after a careless typist made a mistake in 1918. Spell it "Falkner" in all of your school essays, and if your teachers try to correct you, use this as an opportunity to show them how smart you are.

Though Faulkner, after multiple rejections, would eventually be published, he remained relatively obscure from 1926 (publication of his first novel, *Soldiers' Pay*) until his Nobel Prize in Literature in 1949.[2] Back in 1932, in need of money, Faulkner took a deal with MGM Studios to relocate to California and work on screenplays. Ah, California and her glistening sheen, the siren song of money by which a studio can purchase a man's soul.

FAULKNER WORKS YOU NEED TO KNOW

The Sound and the Fury [1929]: A sweeping tragedy that follows the Compson family for thirty years as they fall into financial ruin and disgrace in Mississippi.

As I Lay Dying [1930]: Written in only six weeks, the novel features fifteen different narrators, members of Addie Bundren's family as they plan to bury her. This one is also in Mississippi.

"A Rose for Emily" [1930]: Faulkner's first published story, it is a grotesque (not genre) tale about the funeral of

---

2. Like any true artist, Faulkner did not care for accolades or fame. His own daughter, then seventeen, only learned of his being awarded the Nobel Prize the following day, when she was informed by her high school principal.

an elderly woman in a rural Southern town. A foul smell coming from her bedroom is revealed to be her estranged lover's decaying corpse which she had been sleeping next to for years, and also the stench of the memory of the Civil War (but mostly the dead body).

HOW TO MAKE A MINT JULEP

A mint julep was William Faulkner's signature drink, and if you've been down to his home in Oxford, Mississippi (I have), you'd know they have his julep cup on display alongside his own recipe.

What you need

3 oz. bourbon
1 tsp. sugar
2 sprigs of fresh mint (with additional leaves for garnish)
Crushed ice

In your pewter julep cup that you've kept in the freezer long enough to be frosted, add the sprigs of fresh mint and the teaspoon of sugar. Muddle together. Fill the cup with crushed ice and add your bourbon. Garnish with your fresh mint leaves. Drink on a sleepy afternoon while reclining in a rocking chair on a Mississippi porch, watching the wind rustle the leaves.

SHAKESPEARE PHRASES TO STEAL FOR YOUR BOOK TITLE

"As I lay dying" is a phrase from Homer's *Odyssey*. The title *The Sound and the Fury* is derived from a line from the famous "Tomorrow and tomorrow and tomorrow" soliloquy from Shakespeare's *Macbeth* (". . . Told by an idiot, full of sound and fury, signifying nothing"). Take a clue from Faulkner and use one of these other handy Shakespeare phrases for your next masterpiece:

To Die, to Sleep
From: *Hamlet*
LOGLINE: A Harvard sleep-study scientist begins having dreams of a woman he used to love.

The Wild and Wasteful
From: *Henry V*
LOGLINE: A presidential candidate is forced to relive the debauchery of his Yale fraternity days to address anything that might damage his candidacy. Told mostly through flashbacks.

Crispin Crispian
From: *Henry V*
LOGLINE: A young man named Crispin Crispian moves to Los Angeles and falls in love with a struggling actress/amateur tattoo artist.

This Other Eden
From: *Richard II*
LOGLINE: A dystopian satire about suburban gardens that grow until they literally consume their homeowners. This one might be *Little Shop of Horrors*.

Kill the Envious Moon
From: *Romeo and Juliet*
LOGLINE: Two equally hot women vie for our protagonist's affections. Important: they're hot in different ways. Like, one is brunette and sexy, and the other one is blonde and virtuous. The blonde one wears her hair in a ponytail maybe?

VLADIMIR NABOKOV

THINKING ABOUT COMPLEX IMAGERY

SMARTER THAN EVERYONE (SAME)

Vladimir Nabokov

[1899–1977]

BEST AT LANGUAGES

"Let all of life be an unfettered howl."

Like all great writers, Nabokov was born into a family of esteem and nobility, the type of family for whom a tree graph would require a dozen pages of footnotes and another half dozen pages of endnotes.

Born to a statesman father and an heiress mother, Nabokov grew up in an Elysium usually reserved for fairy tales: a country estate outside of Saint Petersburg, where he learned Russian, English, and French. When he was eighteen, his family fled to Crimea after the October Revolution and later settled in England, where Nabokov would attend Cambridge. Also like something out of a fanciful novel, Nabokov's father was shot in Berlin, assassinated by a Russian monarchist who was actually aiming for someone else. Vladimir's father had been shielding the real target as he was a man of honor.

In Berlin, Nabokov met and married a Russian Jewish woman named Véra, and when she lost her job in 1936 due to mounting anti-Semitism, the couple moved to France, eventually fleeing alongside the entire Nabokov family to America aboard the SS *Champlain*.

Once in America, Nabokov established himself as both an academic and a semiprofessional butterfly scientist. He lectured in comparative literature at

Wellesley—founding their Russian department—and volunteered as an entomologist at the American Museum of Natural History, later becoming a curator at Harvard's Museum of Comparative Zoology. He eventually taught literature at Cornell. What can't this guy do?

FACT

Nabokov's students at Cornell included both Thomas Pynchon and the future Supreme Court justice Ruth Bader Ginsburg, so in many ways, Nabokov is responsible for feminism. Really, how can anyone say that his work is anti-feminist when he taught Ruth Bader Ginsburg? People are so dumb sometimes.

All the while, his wife, Véra, was at his side, working as his secretary, typist, proofreader, editor, translator, agent, manager, legal counsel, research assistant, teaching assistant, chauffeur, and bodyguard—she kept a pistol in her handbag. Never mind the fact that he had an affair when they lived in France, or that he randomly moved their family to Oregon briefly to roam the mountains looking for butterflies. Because, as Nabokov knew, women were best suited to doing whatever it took to support their husbands and absolutely nothing else. "I dislike Jane Austen, and am prejudiced, in fact against all women writers. They are in another class," he wrote to a friend. When he didn't translate his own work, he made it known that he didn't want his translator to be a "Russian-born female." Which is completely understandable, because how would she understand the nuances of fiction *about men*?

"Is this more interesting than my family?"

DID YOU KNOW? (I DID)

Nabokov sometimes snuck himself into his novels. In *Lolita* and *Ada*, there's a character named Vivian Darkbloom, and another, in *King, Queen, Knave*, named Blavdak Vinomori. Both names are anagrams of "Vladimir Nabokov." I have also found subtle ways to insert myself into my own work. In my short story "While the F Train Hums," the philosophy professor has the same last name as me.

NABOKOV WORKS YOU NEED TO KNOW

Speak, Memory [1951]: Nabokov's autobiographical memoir, which concerns his life from childhood up until he emigrated to the United States in 1940. Several of the chapters were previously published elsewhere, including one of the stories, "Mademoiselle O," which was printed in the *Atlantic Monthly* without any indication that it was nonfiction. So, you know, write what you know, especially if what you know is an aristocratic Russian adolescence.

Lolita [1955]: The story's protagonist, Humbert Humbert, is sexually obsessed with underage women he calls nymphets, particularly twelve-year old Dolores "Lolita" Haze, daughter of his landlady (whom he marries to stay close to Lolita). Real art is subversive and edgy, and if your story isn't as shocking as *Lolita*, you probably shouldn't bother.

Pale Fire **(1962):** The title of this surrealist, experimental novel is the name of the poem written by the fictional John Slade, though the bulk of the novel itself is in the foreword and in the commentary by Slade's (also fictional) neighbor sprinkled throughout. It's meta.[1] Bring up *Pale Fire* whenever someone says they like when Deadpool breaks the fourth wall in those inane films they seem to keep making.[2]

THE WHITE MAN'S GUIDE TO EMOJIS

Although nowadays "emojis" are the final refuge of communication for those too obtuse to understand the basic tenets of written language, few people know that the idea of emoticons—using punctuation to evoke a face—originated with Nabokov.

And so although we writers are princes in the

---

1. Making a book or a movie that's meta is the coolest possible thing to do. "Meta" means self-referential, like when a book acknowledges that it's actually a book, or a conversation is *about* how you're having a conversation. It's why every short story I write ends with the main character writing a short story.
2. Or do they? I don't really pay attention to movies. I don't have a TV.

realm of word, not of symbol, in the spirit of Nabokov, it seems worth examining the ways in which emoticons might serve us.

You have no doubt experienced the delights and agonies of writing critiques for the boring and often hack pieces of your fellow writers in a workshop. I have found that simple emoticons provide an easy shorthand to save you valuable time (and save your valuable words for your own creative endeavors).

:]	Promising first effort . . . if you make significant revisions
;]	I see the ways in which you've imitated my own writing, and yes, I will get "coffee" with you after class tomorrow
:]	I'm embarrassed for you
:$	I think your work will find a . . . commercial audience
B[	Derivative of Hunter S. Thompson. Not in a good way.
[:	Clearly influenced by the Japanese storytellers. See? It's right to left.

ERNEST HEMINGWAY

NICE SWOOP

WRITER-CASUAL ATTIRE

RUGGED

Ernest Hemingway

(1899–1961)

MOST LIKELY TO MOVE TO A FOREIGN COUNTRY

"All you have to do is write one true sentence. Write the truest sentence that you know."

Ernest Hemingway was a man's man, and anyone who tells you otherwise is lying. He was born with a full beard and a cable-knit sweater.

Before Hemingway established himself as a writer, he worked as an ambulance driver on the Italian border during the First World War, returning to America long enough to marry his first wife (of four) and bring her with him to Paris, where he sold stories to the *Toronto Star* and developed his voice as a fiction writer. Hemingway drank excessively, surrounded himself with fellow expats, and had as many affairs as he saw fit. His hobbies included shooting animals, dark liquor, wives, war, and restricting expressions of trauma to subtext.

He wrote clean, simple sentences. He did not care for big words. Apocryphally, Faulkner once said Hemingway had "never been known to use a word that might send the reader to the dictionary."

Presumably with hurt feelings, Hemingway replied, "Poor Faulkner. Does he really think big emotions come from big words?" which sounds like a good comeback until you read the rest of the quote, which goes, "He thinks I don't know the ten-dollar words. I know them all right. But there are older and simpler and better words, and those are the ones I use," which is pretty defensive, and just kind of sounds like Hemingway actually maybe doesn't know any ten-dollar words and feels pretty bad about it.

HEMINGWAY WORKS YOU NEED TO KNOW

The Sun Also Rises [1926]: A man who is definitely not Ernest Hemingway is an expatriate who travels from

Paris to Spain to spend time with a group of fellow Americans. Not–Ernest Hemingway has an affair and falls in love with the same woman all of the other Americans have had an affair and fallen in love with. Challenges include: jealous tension, bullfighting, and having to spend time with a Jewish person.

A Farewell to Arms [1929]: War is cruel and senseless, but life is also cruel and senseless. Who's to say whether murdering people is bad? A young American serving as a medic in the Italian forces falls in love with a nurse, who becomes pregnant and then dies in childbirth. We all die. Life is chaos. War is also chaos. Also, it was raining when the nurse died—that's important.

For Whom the Bell Tolls [1940]: War is cruel and senseless (this time it's the Spanish Civil War). An American fighting against fascists in Spain falls in love with a woman, but must leave her for the sake of duty. When the American is mortally wounded after blowing up a bridge, he chooses to wait for the slow agony of death to overtake him, while he uses his remaining time on earth to kill enemy soldiers instead of using his weapon to end his own misery. Death is manly, but not as manly as murdering people in the name of one's country.

The Old Man and the Sea [1952]: Jesus goes out in a boat to try to catch a fish. He eventually catches the fish, and also metaphorically dies for our sins.

A Moveable Feast [1964]: The only important part of *A Moveable Feast*, Hemingway's memoir about his years in Paris, is this scene in which he tries to assure F. Scott Fitzgerald that his manhood isn't too small even though Zelda said it is, and also that women are crazy and are trying to ruin his life.

> *"You're perfectly fine," I said. "You are O.K. There's nothing wrong with you. You look at yourself from above and you look foreshortened. Go over to the Louvre and look at the people in the statues and then go home and look at yourself in the mirror in profile."*

HOW TO DRINK LIKE ERNEST HEMINGWAY

MOJITO

When Hemingway was in Cuba, he drank mojitos, which is *not* a drink for sorority girls or middle-aged women trying to turn a midafternoon lunch at California Pizza Kitchen into a tropical vacation. Mojitos are, in fact, a *very* masculine drink that have been co-opted by the aforementioned groups. Here is how to make one.

What you need

2 tsp. brown sugar
1 lime, juiced
8 fresh mint leaves (plus a sprig for garnish)
1.5 oz. of white rum
Champagne

Add 2 tsp. of brown sugar, the juice of one lime, and eight fresh mint leaves to a high-ball glass. Muddle with the end of a wooden spoon to release all of the mint oil.

Add 1.5 oz. of white rum.

Fill the glass three-fourths of the way full with ice.

Top off with champagne. Hemingway drank his mojitos with champagne, not club soda.

Garnish with a sprig of mint.

ABSINTHE DRIP COCKTAIL

Hemingway was also known to partake in the Green Fairy. We know this because his semiautobiographical character Jake Barnes drinks it a lot in *The Sun Also Rises*.

What you need

Ice water

1.5 oz. absinthe

1 sugar cube

Fill your absinthe fountain with ice water. (You have an absinthe fountain, right? Imagine a tank, with multiple taps coming out.)

Pour the absinthe in your glass, letting the small pool of liquid remind you of the rain on the sidewalk.

Lay your absinthe spoon, topped with the sugar cube, across the rim of the glass like she used to lie across your bed, naked, with the morning light streaming over her limbs. You miss her. She is just a ghost now, a memory.

Let the water from the fountain drip over the sugar cube until the sugar dissolves. Her indent has disappeared from her side of the mattress. Ice water dissolves sugar; time dissolves her memory.

The absinthe should be completely opaque—like her eyes when she told you she couldn't be with you anymore, clouded with regret and impossible to read.

Stir briefly before serving.

FUN FACT

Hemingway also invented his own absinthe-based cocktail, Death in the Afternoon: "Pour one jigger absinthe into a Champagne glass. Add iced Champagne until it attains the proper opalescent milkiness. Drink three to five of these slowly."

JOHN STEINBECK

T-SHIRT + JACKET:
SO LA

John Steinbeck

(1902–1968)

BEST EYES

"Ideas are like rabbits. You get a couple and learn how to handle them, and pretty soon you have a dozen."

We all know that in this new century, the only real writing of any worth is happening in New York City, where artists bundle themselves in scarves against the stale subway air and claw their way into adulthood. New York City is just *real* in a way that the West Coast isn't, you know? But that wasn't always the case. Back in the twentieth century, a man could write decent literature about California. A man, singular. And that man was John Steinbeck.

Born in Salinas, California, Steinbeck went on to attend what some (mistakenly) call the Ivy League of the West Coast,[1] Stanford, although he did not graduate. He also briefly moved to New York to try to make it as a freelance writer, but he couldn't hack it. I get it, John. Not everyone is built for the cunning mistress that is New York City.

Steinbeck married his first wife, Carol Henning, in 1930 and briefly tried to make a living manufacturing plaster mannequins until he was forced to take

---

1. There is no such thing as the Ivy League of the West Coast. That is something parents say when their kids have to go to Pomona.

a different approach: buying a small boat, living off what he could fish and what he could grow in his garden, and sharing his food among friends. If this sounds like communism to you, you are right, and John Steinbeck knew that capitalism is a disease that erodes the human spirit. Have you read Marx? I can lend you my copy, it's somewhere in my dorm room.

All the while, Steinbeck continually wrote about the poor and salt-of-the-earth people in the American West. His novel about migrant workers, *The Grapes of Wrath*, was banned by the powers that be in Kern County—the location where the fictional Joad family ends up in the book—for opening up people's eyes to the evils of terrible labor conditions. Steinbeck wrote, "The vilification of me out here from the large land-owners and bankers is pretty bad. The latest is a rumor started by them that the Okies hate me and have threatened to kill me for lying about them. I'm frightened at the rolling might of this damned thing. It is completely out of hand; I mean a kind of hysteria about the book is growing that is not healthy." That's exactly how I felt when some group on campus protested the publication of my prose poem "Yes I Am White, but I Still Understand Racism Better Than Anyone Else" in the department literary journal.

Steinbeck, like most creatives who should not be expected to give all of themselves to one person forever or even a little bit, married three times. Unfortunately one of those women got on a soapbox and aired her side of the story before he had the chance to write the truth. "Like so many writers, he had several lives, and in each he was spoilt, and in each he felt he was king . . . From the time John awoke to the time he went to bed, I had to be his slave," his second wife, Gwyndolyn Conger, wrote. She called him a "sadistic man," and recounted how he had a rat named Burgess and that "he would let people in and set Burgess loose and gain a great sense of enjoyment, watching people scream and pull up their legs." That last one is a *little* funny. Plus, he won the Nobel Prize, so who really cares what one of his wives thought?

STEINBECK WORKS YOU NEED TO KNOW

Of Mice and Men [1937]: The harrowing and beautiful story of George and Lennie, two migrant field workers in California during the Great Depression. Also, the harrowing story of using rabbits as a euthanasia aid. The title of this one comes from a Robert Burns poem, which is a fine place to look when you run out of Shakespeare quotes.

The Grapes of Wrath [1939]: A realist novel set in the Great Depression about an Oklahoma family, the Joads, trapped in the Dust Bowl, who decide to set out for California. All of that is fine and important, but the real thing you need to take away from this book is that this is the one where a lady breastfeeds an old man at the end.

East of Eden [1952]: A sweeping saga about a family in California. It's a reminder that if you're out of ideas for plot, just take some from the Bible because it's public domain.

JOHN CHEEVER

SINCERELY
POPPED
COLLAR

John Cheever

(1912–1982)

MOST LIKELY TO LEAVE
THE SUBURBS

*"All literary men are Red Sox fans—to be a Yankee
fan in a literate society is to endanger your life."*

The "Chekhov of the suburbs" is famous for both his short stories and his tortured bisexuality. Oh, and his rampant alcoholism. See, one thing that Cheever knew is that part of being a writer is projecting all of your inner demons on the people closest to you and then drinking until the world becomes a painful, anesthetized blur. There is no better cure for self-loathing than giving your wife the silent treatment for days or disappearing from your family altogether for long stretches of time in order to go on a bender. That's just what artists *do*. Ask Cheever's good friend John Updike about it. John Updike knows.

In the '60s, Cheever was at the height of his career: the *New York Times* lovingly dubbed him the "Ovid of Ossining" (the suburb where he lived with his wife, Mary, and their three children), *The New Yorker* published his acclaimed story "The Swimmer," and Burt Lancaster was set to star in the film adaptation. But like any real artist, Cheever wasn't going to let "success" get in the way of being a tortured alcoholic.

Cheever blamed Mary for the decline of their marriage and his deteriorating mental state, telling his psychiatrist that she was hostile and dark. Of course he was right—Mary wasn't properly supporting his craft. The psychiatrist called Mary in for a joint session, and apparently that hack thought *Cheever* was the one to blame. As Cheever wrote in his journal, the doctor said he was "a neurotic man, narcissistic, egocentric, friendless, and so deeply involved in [his] own defensive illusions that [he has] invented a manic-depressive wife." The man was a fraud, clearly, and Cheever ended his therapy. Also, he had an affair with the actress Hope Lange.

When you're a genius, drinking heavily and lashing out at those who love you with endless and unearned patience is a quirk and a sign of tortured thoughts bubbling underneath the surface! Besides, after he almost died from a pulmonary edema due to heavy drinking, Cheever got clean after only one or two or three more drinking-to-suicidal-level relapses.

CHEEVER WORKS YOU NEED TO KNOW

"The Five-Forty-Eight" (1954): A businessman in New York City catches the five-forty-eight train home while trying to escape Miss Dent, his former secretary, whom he fired after their one-night stand. She threatens him at gunpoint and then lets him go. At gunpoint!

"The Swimmer" (1964): A man named Neddy Merrill lounging at a friend's pool whimsically decides he'll make his way home by taking a dip in all of the neighbors' pools along the way. As he swims on, the story becomes surreal; his friends all seem to be in decline, it's unclear how much time has passed, and the season might be autumn (or fall, to those in the Midwest). Strangest of all, some of the lower-income neighbors even act like they don't want Neddy jumping over their fences and swimming through their pools. Hard to make sense of this at first, but read it three to four times and let's talk.

Bullet Park [1969]: A loving father named Eliot Nailles is fatefully bound to his neighbor, a psychotic man named Hammer,[1] but what he really has to face is the emptiness of suburbia. Do you get it? His name is Nailles and the other guy's name is Hammer. See, it's that sort of reference that most casual readers don't really pick up on.

Falconer [1977]: A former university professor is in prison for the murder of his brother and begins an affair (no homo) with a fellow prisoner.

---

1. Get it?

Saul Bellow

(1915–2005)

MOST FASHIONABLE

"Women are the rails on which men run."

Even though he was technically born in Canada like some sort of weak-minded doughnut-eating idiot, Saul Bellow is still one of America's most important writers, celebrated for his ability to capture postwar spiritual alienation and look good doing it. No, really. After his first novel came out, MGM saw his author photo and called to inquire whether he might be interested in being in the movies as the type of guy who would lose the girl to an actor with a more classic "leading man" look like Errol Flynn.

That is the bar against which you should set your pathetic author photo.

The face on the inside book jacket should be suave and handsome enough for a major Hollywood studio to want to get in touch, but not so overly good-looking to suggest he is cruising by on some genetic fortune. Artists are hot *because* of their talent, not despite it.

Intelligent enough to recognize that his talent was best left untarnished by the shallow, tawdry world of Hollywood, Bellow instead devoted his life to letters.

His Jewish family settled in Chicago when he was young, and Bellow would go on to study anthropology and sociology at the University of Chicago and Northwestern.[1] After serving as a merchant marine, he went on to teach intellectual history at a number of colleges throughout his life, but all the while he quietly continued to write at night, facing rejection after rejection but continuing to produce because he had to write—it wasn't a choice; writing was his lifeline. You understand.

Bellow didn't hit it big as an author until *Herzog*, published when he was forty-nine years old, but from then on, Bellow's talents were justly recognized. He would go on to win the Nobel Prize, the Pulitzer, and the National Book Award (three times for that last one, no big deal). He also married five times because when you're brilliant and handsome you shouldn't have to restrict yourself to just one marriage.

Being brilliant and handsome also means you're allowed to do what Bellow did when faced with criticism, which is: cut said person out of your life and/or claim it was part of an elaborate conspiracy theory. Sometimes his *complex* personality meant people misunderstood him: like, in an interview, when Bellow said, "Who is the Tolstoy of the Zulus, the Proust of the Papuans?" I mean, wow. I almost

---

1. People may tell you these schools are the "Ivy League of the Midwest," which isn't true, because the Ivy League of the Midwest is made up and an oxymoron.

signed up for a gender studies seminar my freshman year, and so I can recognize when guys like Bellow say screwed-up stuff. This is the sort of thing I'll tweet about so people who follow me recognize how sensitive and worldly I am. My voice needs to be heard on the important issues! Of course I'm already drafting an op-ed in my head for when that PC stuff goes too far.

BELLOW WORKS YOU NEED TO KNOW

The Adventures of Augie March [1953]: One of the Great American Novels. A young man matures, from childhood to adulthood, while trying to find meaning

and self-discovery by having affairs with a string of assorted women.

Herzog [1964]: In this novel mostly told through letters, a man named Herzog is having a midlife crisis after two divorces, and even a relationship with a beautiful and vibrant younger woman can't help.

J. D. SALINGER

PHONY DETECTOR

INTELLECTUAL JACKET

J. D. Salinger

(1919–2010)

LEAST SOCIAL

"An artist's only concern is to shoot for some kind of perfection, and on his own terms, not anyone else's."

I know pretty much everything about notoriously private J. D. Salinger's life (Uncle Sal, if you must know), but I promised I wouldn't go into too much detail because he really did value his privacy. (That's the sort of thing you learn pretty quickly about Uncle Sal.)

Like many of the best tortured literary minds of the twentieth century, Salinger was Jewish and he grew up in New York City, within that glittering concrete prison of phonies and fakes. Before serving in World War II, he studied at Ursinus College and Columbia University, getting a few short stories published before he was drafted into the army. Overseas, he fought on D-Day and in the Battle of the Bulge, but more importantly, he befriended Ernest Hemingway.

Upon returning to the United States—with a daughter and a failed marriage—Salinger continued publishing short stories. He also got very into Zen Buddhism, to the point where he would bring along a reading list for any lucky lady who found herself on a date with him. This is an important takeaway for you here: that is something you should absolutely be doing on every single one of your dates. They love it. And they are grateful for the introduction to the ideas.

At age thirty-six, he married a college student at Radcliffe named Claire Douglas, and insisted that she drop out of school before graduation and live with him, which of course she did because being in such proximity to Salinger was obviously an amazing opportunity. (This was a step up from when he dated Oona O'Neill—daughter of Eugene, future wife of Charlie Chaplin—when she was underage and in high school and Salinger was in his twenties.)

The always philosophically minded Salinger was briefly interested in Dianetics (the forerunner to Scientology), but he had a longer relationship with Christian Science, which is why he refused to take his infant daughter Margaret to the doctor when she was sick.

CAREER ADVICE

When it came to his short stories, Salinger famously refused to be edited, and he insisted that editors not change a single word of his writing. This is the approach any real artist should take. In fact, much of my most pointed commentary has been struck from these pages by a commercial entity not interested in sharing my point of view in its purest form. This is why the book feels so incredibly polished and unlike my raw-edged self you might have encountered if *Tin House* had ever published my stuff.

After the monumental success of *The Catcher in the Rye*, his first and only novel, Salinger retreated from public life, which means that he and Claire lived in Cornish, New Hampshire, together, relatively isolated from the rest of the world. Well, when I say "together," I mean when Salinger wasn't on his own, recharging creatively for weeks-long stretches to work on a story and also come back with a new religion.

But when, isolated from her friends and family, Claire couldn't take the creative life and became lonely and decided to separate from and divorce Salinger, things still ended up okay: he started a relationship with the eighteen-year-old Joyce Maynard, who had become a minor celebrity after a celebrated essay of hers was published in the *New York Times*. Upgrade. After reading the essay in question, Salinger initiated correspondence with a letter, and eventually Maynard dropped out of Yale and forwent her scholarship to live with Salinger for exactly ten months. Salinger writing letters to much-younger women was very much his MO. It's actually how he met his final wife, whom he married when he was seventy and she was thirty.

Salinger preferred his protagonists, like his wives, young, full of life before corruption by the bitter world of capitalism and compromise and older, predatory men.

SALINGER WORKS YOU NEED TO KNOW

"A Perfect Day for Bananafish" [1948]: A newlywed man meets a pure child on the beach while his wife is talking on the phone in their hotel room, and then he kills himself because all women are shrews unless they're children.

"For Esmé—with Love and Squalor" [1950]: A young British orphaned child meets an American soldier during World War II and is able to sense his depth and loneliness because she is mature for her age and because there is nothing purer than friendships between adult men and children.

The Catcher in the Rye [1951]**:** Our hero, Holden Caulfield, is a student who's young, yes, but old enough to know that everyone around him is a phony, except his little sister and his little brother who died.

HOW TO SPOT A PHONY

He talks about "summering" and "going to the country club" and "skiing" and "enjoying the holidays at home with his family."

His dad went to the same prep school as him.

He says he likes the White Stripes or the Rolling Stones, but he can't even name his top fifteen songs in order.

He's on some sports team or whatever.

He hasn't even read the works of J. D. Salinger.

HOW TO DISAPPEAR FOREVER, PART 1

If you really want to go off the grid for good, it's going to take more than just deleting your Facebook account. First, you're going to want to get rid of your iPhone or your smartphone of choice (it's an iPhone). Wait until your phone is completely drained of battery—six to seven hours, most likely—and then find the nearest large body of water. Using your shoelace, secure a large rock to your phone, and throw it as far as you can into the water. Admire the ripples as your beloved sinks, and think of how nice it would be to take a picture of those ripples and upload it to Instagram, maybe in black and white? Wait, fuck, hold on, we forgot to take out the SIM card—even if the phone is at the bottom of the lake, there's no telling what people could recover from that. So strip down to your underwear, and using whatever rudimentary diving equipment you can procure, get into the water and find the iPhone at the bottom of the lake. Now, once you bring it back to shore, use a safety pin or paper clip to pry open the SIM card slot on the side of the phone. Keep that safe for now while you tie another rock to your phone using your other shoelace and then fling it back into the murky depths below.

Now, with your SIM card: bring it home and, using a hammer, break it into even smaller pieces. But even that's not going to be enough to keep the government from being able to track you. What you're going to want to do now is get out your blender. Blend the remains of the SIM card into a fine powder. Add cold brew, protein powder, and one semi-rotten banana that you forgot you had in the back of your fridge. Blend together and drink in one long swig. Your stomach acids will inactivate the card's tracking capabilities, and you'll harmlessly pass its remains over the next few days.

CHARLES BUKOWSKI

A BEANIE!!! FINALLY.

GREAT ARTISTS DON'T HAVE TIME TO "SHOWER" OR "NOT LOOK LIKE SHIT"

Charles Bukowski

(1920–1994)

MOST LIKELY TO GET EXPELLED

"How the hell could a person enjoy being awakened at 6:30 AM, by an alarm clock, leap out of bed, dress, force-feed, shit, piss, brush teeth and hair, and fight traffic to get to a place where essentially you made lots of money for somebody else and were asked to be grateful for the opportunity to do so?"

Charles Bukowski is the American underground, the counterculture. He is the commune of bums beneath a bridge sharing booze and poetry, the filthy bathroom stalls in a rock club at 4 AM, a used condom dangling from a highway overpass, warm beer, aging whores, forgotten love, and whiskey-addled memories. Maybe also misogyny, but mostly just the aforementioned counterculture stuff.

Born in Germany but raised in Los Angeles, Bukowski's life was a series of odd jobs. On the list: dishwasher, truck driver, mailman, gas station attendant, bull wrangler, Red Cross orderly, elevator operator, tap dancer, dog-biscuit factory worker, slaughterhouse worker, mall Santa Claus, and lobster fisherman. I only made up four of those, and even the ones I made up are probably true. That's how kooky he was.

Bukowski began writing in earnest after ten years of heavy drinking when a bleeding ulcer meant a near-death experience. His poetry was raw, talked about real-life situations, like getting drunk, or getting drunk while down at the racetrack and meeting ladies of the night you'll come to regret keeping company with. You know those robots who think poetry has to rhyme or has to be about feminine garbage like flowers or sunsets? Show them some Bukowski. Now that's a guy who gets human nature.

HOW TO DATE LIKE BUKOWSKI

[D]on't wait for the good woman. She doesn't exist. There are women who can make you feel more with their bodies and their souls but these are the exact women who will turn the knife into you right in front of the crowd. Of course, I expect this, but the knife still cuts. The female loves to play man against man, and if she is in a position to do it there is not one who will not resist. The male, for all his bravado and exploration, is the loyal one, the one who generally feels love. The female is skilled at betrayal and torture and damnation. Never envy a man his lady. Behind it all lays a living hell.

PICTURED: A WOMAN

BUKOWSKI WORKS YOU NEED TO KNOW

Post Office [1971]: Bukowski's first novel is about a man named Henry Chinaski who drinks, gambles, and sleeps with women in between working as a mail carrier. It was published when he was fifty, so if you, like me, have already written four—as *yet* unpublished—manuscripts, then you're ahead of the game.

Factotum [1975]: Another Henry Chinaski novel, this time about him drunkenly and aimlessly wandering Los Angeles, getting rejected by a publisher even though he's way more talented than the lazy sycophants they're publishing. He falls in love with a woman who leaves him, and then has a fling with a gold-digging floozy. No one understands him.

Ham on Rye [1982]: A coming-of-age novel about Henry Chinaski, about him dealing with his abusive father and ineffectual mother and discovering masturbation and alcohol. As he grows up, he becomes increasingly disillusioned by the American Dream. The only solution is more masturbation and alcohol.

HOW TO MAKE A BOILERMAKER

Bukowski's drink of choice didn't involve any fancy stemmed glassware. There are no juices or infusions or essences. It is a simple drink for a man at the end of a long day's work (work he probably did with his hands). A boilermaker, a.k.a. a beer and a shot, is exactly the thing you order to prove that you're not messing around when it comes to transgressive fiction *or* alcohol.

What you need

3 oz. bourbon or rye whiskey
12 oz. beer

Drink the shot of whiskey, and then chase it with your beer. Do not drop your whiskey into your beer unless you live like a former frat bro turned stockbroker.

Jack Kerouac

(1922–1969)

MOST LIKELY TO LIVE IN AN RV

"Avoid the world, it's just a lot of dust and drag and means nothing in the end."

As someone who prefers to listen to music on vinyl, I consider myself a kindred spirit with the Beat Generation, those artists who captured the lonely burden of living in a changing nation the way only an Ivy League education can teach you. A lifelong responsibility and a curse!

Kerouac's family was French Canadian, and he didn't even learn English until he was six, after already being fluent in French, which explains some of the lyricism in his language. If you don't speak at least two languages, there's no way you can appreciate the subtleties of Kerouac's talent. And those talents weren't just limited to writing: he was a football player, which brought him to Columbia, where he played until he broke his leg, could no longer play, and thus dropped out. But he continued to live on the Upper West Side and cavort with Allen Ginsberg and Lucien Carr, who were busy reciting French poetry denying the whiff of homosexual scandal.

Kerouac's most famous work, *On the Road*, was written on a single, unbroken 120-foot scroll made of sheets of drafting paper that Kerouac had taped together so that he could feed it, uninterrupted, into his typewriter. You know when you're working on something so incredible that the merest interruption—even adding a new piece of paper to your typewriter—could disrupt the fragile alchemy of literary brilliance? Yep. That's what happened here. The final draft took only twenty days (incredible), during which he wrote continuously while his wife, Joan, supplied him with the coffee, Benzedrine, cigarettes, and bowls of soup that he needed and deserved in order to keep him going.

Speaking of Joan, perhaps even more experimental than Kerouac's writing methods was his personal life. For years he lived inside a performance piece that most art historians have yet to recognize—something I have been privately calling "getting divorced from your pregnant wife and not acknowledging your daughter for nine years until a blood test confirms she is actually yours." This was and remains a truly groundbreaking dissection of the American family. What I think of when I think of jazz poetry.

KEROUAC WORKS YOU NEED TO KNOW

On the Road [1957]: A largely autobiographical book in which characters "Sal Paradise" and "Dean Moriarty" are stand-ins for Kerouac and Neal Cassady. The two go on a road trip to explore America and to just *live*, you know?

The Dharma Bums [1958]: This one is also autobiographical, about "Ray Smith" (Jack Kerouac) and "Japhy Ryder" (Gary Snyder) as the two of them have conversations about the outdoors and hitchhiking and America and jazz while "Ray" attempts to understand Buddhism.

Big Sur [1962]: This time Kerouac's name is Jack Duluoz and Cassady is Cody Pomeray. But very, VERY different from *On the Road* and well worth reading two to four times. Note: these are also the same fake names Kerouac uses in his semiautobiographical novel *Desolation Angels*. It's easy to get confused.

HOW TO MAKE A MARGARITA

Frequently traveling to Mexico meant that Kerouac got a taste for mezcal, and his cocktail of choice was the margarita. Don't expect sugar rims or watermelon flavoring here; this is a manly drink for men who want to drive south of the border and get so drunk so often that their family and friends will intervene because it has become a massive problem.

What you need
_____

1.5 oz. tequila
1 oz. triple sec
0.5 oz. fresh lime juice

Run a slice of lime around the edge of your glass.

Shake together all of the ingredients over ice, and don't bother to strain it. Pour the drink, ice and all, into your glass, and enjoy.

HOW TO ORDER COFFEE

Bleary eyes, insaned mind bemused and mystified by sleep, details that pop out even as you write them you don't know what they mean, till you wake up, have coffee, look at it, and see the logic of dreams in dream language itself, see?

—Book of Dreams

For the record, Kerouac drank his own coffee black and—especially while writing *On the Road*—in massive quantities.

Espresso

To be sipped while sitting in the window of the coffee shop, adjusting your glasses and rubbing your chin.

Flat White

Only if you've been to Australia and can confidently shake your head and say, "Yeah, they just don't make them here correctly."

Caffe Latte

For the weak or infirm.

Caffe Breve

An indulgence, only to be consumed in celebration of winning the MacArthur genius grant.

Cappuccino

Acceptable while lingering at a table in an Italian piazza enjoying the last of the late afternoon sun.

Caffe Mocha

A drink for a child.

Drip Coffee

Take it black, and work that into conversation as often as possible.

Americano

The sophisticated choice, for when you've upgraded your sneakers to Chelsea boots. The Warby Parker of coffee drinks.

Tea

For Jane Austen readers and the English, who haven't managed to produce a groundbreaking novel in 80 years.

KURT VONNEGUT

THE '70S IN ONE PICTURE

Kurt Vonnegut

(1922–2007)

MOST DEPENDABLE

"Everything was beautiful and nothing hurt."

Now, normally I don't go for genre writers. Genre is the refuge of those unskilled enough to illuminate the details and contradictions of our own bleary lives. And so, since they aren't insightful enough to do as I do—last year, for instance, I wrote a 14,000-word short story from the perspective of a melting ice cube in a glass of whiskey—some "authors" write tales about magic and giants or whatnot. Children's stories.

But I do think—and yes, I am the first to make this judgment—it is appropriate to make an exception for Kurt Vonnegut, whose darkly humorous anti-war novels, while sometimes *slightly science fiction*, still illuminate profound truths of Mankind.

HAHAHA I'LL EXPLAIN LATER

The highlights of Vonnegut's life are not academic: the writer was placed on academic probation at Cornell for poor grades and dropped out, enlisting in the army to fight in World War II. Later, after he returned from the war, he would also leave the University of Chicago without a degree when his thesis was unanimously rejected by the board. It just goes to show you that a literary mind cannot be contained by the constraints of academic evaluation. So even if your freshman-year literature professor at Harvard gives you a D because he doesn't think you "comprehended, or even actually read" *Pride and Prejudice*, it doesn't matter. In fact, it means you're something like beloved American author Kurt Vonnegut.

His wartime experience, particularly as a prisoner of war during the bombing of Dresden, later inspired his most seminal work, *Slaughterhouse-Five*, which would inspire me to force a group of students who hadn't read the book to forgo Berlin for Dresden on our free weekend in Germany. They eventually thanked me, of course. So while many talk about this book after having read it only once, I must say, personally, I tend to favor the slightly more obscure *Breakfast of Champions*. Four of my tattoos are Vonnegut's illustrations from that book, including the one shown on page 164. I won't tell you what it is; you'd get it if you read the book.

VONNEGUT WORKS YOU NEED TO KNOW

The Sirens of Titan [1959]: I'm an atheist, so "Church of God the Utterly Indifferent" is actually really funny satire to me.

Cat's Cradle [1963]: The arms race will be even more terrible if people figure out how to weaponize ice-creation technology.

Slaughterhouse-Five [1969]: Our protagonist, Billy Pilgrim, becomes unstuck in time in a nonlinear story about a soldier who becomes a prisoner of war in Dresden, survives the firebombing, and then is kidnapped as an exhibition in an alien zoo. Relatable, if you think about it.

HOW TO DEAL WITH REJECTION LETTERS

In 1949, Vonnegut submitted three samples to *Atlantic Monthly* and received the following reply:

> *We have been carrying out our usual summer house-cleaning of the manuscripts on our anxious bench and in the file, and among them I find the three papers which you have shown me as samples*

of your work. I am sincerely sorry that no one of them seems to us well adapted for our purpose. Both the account of the bombing of Dresden and your article, "What's a Fair Price for Golden Eggs?" have drawn commendation although neither one is quite compelling enough for final acceptance.

Of course that "account of the bombing of Dresden" would be further developed into *Slaughterhouse-Five*.

Here are a few suggestions on how best to deal with your own meaningless rejection letters from the simpering elitist know-nothings who have installed themselves at prestigious publications:

1. Create a sculpture using papier-mâché. Every man needs a life-size bust of himself made of paper and glue in his room.

2. Cut out phrases and rearrange them into a new poem. Leave copies of the poem on tables at your local coffee shop for customers to find.

3. Take the letters to a secluded wooded location and use them as kindling for a bonfire. Watch the flames dance and lick at the night sky. Sit until the fire burns itself into orange embers, bright and luminous like the eyes of some mythical beast.

4. Carefully use the rejection letters to make hand-rolled cigarettes.

5. Leave in library books as an ambitious, ambiguous public art project.

6. Do a dramatic reading of each letter as a monologue at your university's open mic night.

7. Tear the letters into pieces and sprinkle them onto a lake at dawn.

8. Build paper airplanes to remind you of the innocence of youth. As the airplanes descend, remember that we must all grow old and die.

9. Crumple the letters into stress balls to squeeze to help relieve symptoms of carpal tunnel from hours spent at your typewriter.

10. Post them up around your desk as a reminder that your work is too sophisticated and complex for mainstream consumption.

NORMAN MAILER

GREAT MUSS!

JUST A WHITE T? IS THERE ANYTHING COOLER?! (NO.)

Norman Mailer

(1923–2007)

DEVIL IN DISGUISE

"We must face the simple fact that maybe there's a profound reservoir of cowardness in women that had them welcome this miserable, slavish life."

There's a lot of confusion around about Norman Mailer's personal life: Did he once stab his wife in the heart at a party and almost kill her (only receiving three years' probation)? Did he once punch another of his wives while she was six months pregnant? Who can ever know!

Here's some of what we do know: Mailer was born in New Jersey and enrolled in Harvard when he was sixteen years old. For some godforsaken reason, his draft deferment was denied when Mailer said he was writing "important literary work," and so Mailer served until 1947. He completed a French language course at the University of Paris and returned to the US, where he would go on to have eleven bestselling books and six wives.

A champion of the avant-garde and clearly a "Team NYC" member of the MFA vs. NYC debate, Mailer was one of the founders of the *Village Voice*.

MAILER WORKS YOU NEED TO KNOW

The Naked and the Dead [1948]: Based on Mailer's experience during World War II, the novel is an epic four-part narrative about a platoon on a fictional South Pacific island named Anopopei, where soldiers presumably try to murder the opposing forces and not their wives.

The Executioner's Song [1979]: A Pulitzer Prize–winning novel about the execution of Gary Gilmore in Utah, a true-crime story that, as of this writing, has not yet been turned into a podcast.

An American Dream [1965]: Our hero, Rojack, gets drunk at a party, strangles his estranged wife, makes it look like a suicide, then rapes her maid. He goes on to experience the seedy underbelly of the Manhattan jazz scene and has lots of sex with a mobster's girlfriend, because he is the American Dream.

HOW TO HAND-ROLL A CIGARETTE

Not only are cigarettes you roll yourself cheaper than their drugstore equivalent, they also let people know that you met a girl in France named Mathilde and she taught you how to do so as the sun came up. Scratch that. Tell people that you taught Mathilde.

1. Fold the rolling paper vertically to form a skinny V, a gutter for the tobacco to collect. Hold it in your left hand with your index finger inside the V and your thumb and middle finger to brace it on the outside.

2. If you're using a filter, drop it into the gutter and let it slide down to the left side, underneath your index finger.

3. Sprinkle about a half-dollar-size amount of shredded tobacco into the rolling paper and spread it evenly along the V gutter. The tobacco should end right at your finger, where the filter begins.

4. Gently push the tobacco down, compressing it into a tight log.

5. Fold the V up with the tobacco inside, and rub it back and forth between your fingers so the tobacco becomes a tighter log within the paper.

You should be using both of your hands, rubbing the tops of the paper just where they overlap, between your thumbs and forefingers. It might take five to ten rockings or more for the tobacco to settle into a solid cylinder.

6. The actual rolling:

Roll one side of the paper downward so that its edge is flush with the tobacco. It might take some practice, but the goal is to tuck that paper underneath the tobacco log so you can begin rolling up the paper as tightly as possible. With your thumbs holding the bottom of the paper-wrapped tobacco stable, push the top paper side over the log, and roll upward.

7. Lick the gum strip at the top of the paper and seal your cigarette.

8. Wait for a few moments for the glue to dry.

9. Light it.

10. Sit on a bench and stare contemplatively into the distance. If anyone tries to interact with you, just soberly shake your head and continue gazing.

JOHN UPDIKE

TURTLENECK—
AND-JACKET COMBO
IS A MASTER CLASS

John Updike

(1932–2009)

BIGGEST GOSSIP

"Most of American life consists of driving somewhere and then returning home, wondering why the hell you went."

Thank god for John Updike, the man finally brave enough to tell the story of white, middle-class American Protestants struggling with issues that ranged from the temptation to commit adultery to committing adultery. One of our nation's most prolific authors, Updike churned out about a book a year—and none of that James Patterson garbage, because John Updike won the Nobel Prize in Literature *twice*.

When he was a student at Harvard, Updike was a star writer for the *Harvard Lampoon*, but seeing as it was too early for him to get a job writing on *The Simpsons*, he instead went to work at *The New Yorker*, where he published his early short stories and built a name for himself as a giant of the literary community.

Some people are ill-informed enough to think that Updike was a sexist because he almost constantly wrote about adultery and described women's bodies and general appearances in his novels with a mocking judgmental tone and with a near-militaristic attention to the very moment they become too old to be pretty anymore (hint: thirty-three). Those people clearly forget that Updike wrote the novel *The Witches of Eastwick*, which is a book entirely devoted to *witches*, i.e., women.

UPDIKE WORKS YOU NEED TO KNOW

THE RABBIT SERIES

Rabbit, Run [1960]: Former high school basketball star Harry "Rabbit" Angstrom is trapped in a meaningless suburban existence with his pregnant wife, infant child, and boring job. He tries to escape, but just has an affair instead. He comes back when his wife goes into labor, though, which is nice of him, but then his wife refuses to have sex with him after giving birth. And so Harry leaves and goes back to his mistress. His crazy wife accidentally drowns their infant in the tub, though, so Harry is forced to come back home. He finds out his mistress is pregnant, but he's not going to leave his wife, so he abandons the pregnant mistress. She knew what this was.

Rabbit Redux [1971]: In the sequel, Janice leaves Harry, and Harry, having reached the tragic middle age of thirty-six, reevaluates his life. He forms a commune with a cynical Vietnam vet and a rich, runaway teenage girl, and the three of them have sex and do drugs until a disgruntled conservative neighbor burns their house down. The teenage girl burns to death, but it's really a tragedy for Harry. His wife comes back to him.

Rabbit Is Rich (1981): Having inherited his wife's father's Toyota dealership, Harry is finally financially stable, but he's still not happy.

Rabbit at Rest (1990): Harry has retired to Florida with his wife, but he's still unhappy. He has heart surgery and recognizes the nurse as his possible illegitimate daughter. He doesn't say anything. Harry's long-term mistress dies, and at the funeral he sees that a woman he was once attracted to has become obese and unattractive. Harry's wife discovers that Harry had a one-night-stand with their son's wife. Harry runs back to Florida and has a heart attack and dies. Such is life.

The Witches of Eastwick (1984): Three witches in a coven in a fictional Rhode Island town all fall in love with the same mysterious stranger named Darryl who comes to town. All is more or less okay until Darryl marries a young, beautiful woman in the town and sets the witches off into a jealous frenzy. They give the young woman magical cancer, and she dies, and Darryl flees. The book is very feminist, and if anyone thinks it's patriarchal that women need a man in order to come into their full powers, just remind them that this book is a *parody* of that traditional narrative, probably.

HOW TO WRITE A FEMALE CHARACTER

1. Describe her physically.

Female characters must always be willowy, with graceful necks and slender arms and long, preferably auburn, hair. Raven hair can do in a pinch. Her eyes are either startlingly green or muddied green, depending on whether she will make your protagonist Happy or Sad. When she has sex with your protagonist, use that as an opportunity to describe her ivory skin and freckles. If a woman is unattractive, find out exactly what is wrong with her and zero in on it with precision: Are her legs too thick? Does her upper lip sprout a few blonde hairs? Or are her eyes just weighted with an exhaustion that has sucked away their youthful light and glow?

2. Give her a personality.

   She likes to drink, maybe too much, but most of the time your protagonist likes drinking with her. She seems tough, but she has a vulnerable side only your protagonist can see. She's promiscuous and her smiles are always mischievous, unless she is your protagonist's wife, in which case she hasn't had sex or smiled in one hundred years.

3. Give her a character arc.

   Just kidding.

KNOW THE DIFFERENCE: IS SHE AN EX-WIFE OR AN INGENUE?

(HINT: Does she want to sleep with you?)

EX-WIFE

INGENUE

SEVERE GAZE

PRETTY BUT MEAN

LET HERSELF GO

YOUNG AND SMALL

BRIGHT

CHEERY

PHILIP ROTH

STRONG WRITER BROWS

HE'S THE (ZUCKER) MAN!
I'LL EXPLAIN LATER.

Philip Roth

(1933–2018)

MOST LIKELY TO WIN
THE NOBEL PRIZE

"The road to hell is paved with works-in-progress."

According to legend, every year on the day the Nobel Prize in Literature was to be announced, Philip Roth would put on a suit, take the train to Manhattan, and sit in his agent's office, at a desk with a press schedule already planned out and a phone that was to ring any second now. He never won the Nobel Prize. On the year that the Nobel committee had to forgo a prize due to sexual misconduct within its ranks, Roth died (for reasons they claimed were unrelated, but which were probably related).

If you don't count Woody Allen, Philip Roth is perhaps the best voice of middle-class American Jewish ennui. He overcame the metaphorical *A* on his chest of being born in New Jersey to emerge as a giant on the literary landscape, the only novelist with the bravery required to write about masturbating with a piece of liver.[1]

Roth's writing career took place mostly in the hallowed halls of academia; he was awarded his master's in English literature from the University of

---

1. Most people don't realize *American Pie* is actually loosely based on *Portnoy's Complaint*.

Chicago, went on to teach creative writing at Iowa and Princeton, and eventually taught comparative literature at University of Pennsylvania until he retired in 1991.

When women write fiction, it's about them. Trust me—ask any female novelist. Philip Roth, on the other hand, is a respected literary titan, and his alter ego, Nathan Zuckerman, a Jewish man from New York (who appears in a number of novels and novellas), is a brilliant *subversion* of that.

Roth won the National Book Award for his first book, *Goodbye, Columbus*, which is an accolade many have predicted I, too, will share as soon as the mainstream publishers find the courage to print my 110,000-word experimental novel, *When Cigarette Smoke Becomes Its Own Ash*.

ROTH WORKS YOU NEED TO KNOW

Portnoy's Complaint [1969]: Written entirely as a monologue delivered by Portnoy while he's in therapy, this is the urtext for any and all depictions of a Jewish mother. Chances are, nothing you've ever said in therapy is as interesting or as important as this.

American Pastoral [1997]: Roth's alter ego, Nathan Zuckerman, narrates this story about a recently deceased former classmate named Seymour "Swede" Levov, who died because the American Dream is in turmoil. People are dying! That's not the America we were promised!

CORMAC MCCARTHY

EYES SPARKLE WITH LITERARY POSSIBILITY

THAT SMILE!

Cormac McCarthy

[1933–]

MOST LIKELY TO WIN AN OSCAR

"Deep in each man is the knowledge that something knows of his existence. Something knows, and cannot be fled nor hid from."

Cormac McCarthy doesn't write about trivial garbage. He writes about life and death. He has no need for punctuation, which only slows down a sentence as it unfurls its simple but profound truths unto the reader. When you want to write like Cormac McCarthy you must remember that semicolons are for women and the French. Do not abide by their neither-here-nor-there nonsense. Either end a sentence or don't, but by god make a decision.

TITULAR TIDBIT

Though his birth name is actually Charles, he changed it to Cormac for the purposes of his writing career to honor the Irish high kings and also because there was a famous ventriloquist dummy named Charlie McCarthy.

Instead of wasting his time on some ivory-tower college degree, McCarthy lived with his first wife in a shack in the foothills of the Smoky Mountains, a shack without heat or running water. *That*, my friends, is how you learn to be a great writer. It's through struggle, i.e., the struggle to keep yourself warm and take a shower. Poverty is noble and, when you think about it, a gift for creativity.

After his first divorce, McCarthy moved to Texas, where he reinvented the Western novel, writing dense and bloody philosophical scenes about people being scalped and murdered that really you probably won't be able to understand on first or even third readings. The vitality and brilliance of his prose are a lot for most people.

Although he cautiously guards his privacy, he did agree to a televised interview with Oprah in 2007, when his novel *The Road* was selected for her pandering book club. In the interview Cormac revealed that he is only friends with scientists and doesn't know any other writers. This is a really interesting thing about him, and proves he has absolutely no skin in the literary game. He's actually just pure genius.

He married his third wife, thirty-two years his junior, in 1997, and although they have since divorced (probably because she couldn't understand him), McCarthy—now in his mid-eighties—has a son born in 1999 which just goes to show the depth of his manly vitality.

McCARTHY WORKS YOU NEED TO KNOW

Blood Meridian (1985): A gang of villains led by Judge Holden scalp Native Americans across the West. The red dirt, like man, is evil.

No Country for Old Men (2005): Oh, have they made this one into a movie? I hadn't heard.

The Road (2006): A postapocalyptic novel about a father and son journeying across the country after an extinction event, trying to survive. But death is inevitable. Humanity is corrupted.

HOW TO CHOOSE A WRITING INSTRUMENT AND WHAT IT SAYS ABOUT YOU

Cormac McCarthy purchased a powder blue Olivetti Lettera 32 mechanical typewriter in a Tennessee pawnshop in 1963, for fifty dollars, and used it for the next five decades, producing an estimated five million words tickling its ivories. An author's instrument is more than tool; it is an extension of his very soul. With that in mind, choose your weapon carefully.[1]

---

1. I use the Olivetti Lettera 22 (the earlier model) myself.

Ballpoint pen: Let me guess. You probably have a great idea for a book that you've been meaning to write but haven't actually got around to starting.

Fountain pen: You don't use contractions because you think they degrade the language, and your epigraphs are all in Latin. You include epigraphs for everything you write.

Electric typewriter: All of your protagonists are thinly veiled versions of yourself. You order rye at bars and secretly think you should have been alive in the '60s.

Manual typewriter: You spent $600 on a typewriter that you've used twice.

No. 2 pencil: You keep one behind your ear because you think it looks writerly, but you really only use it to jot down to-do lists.

Pencil you can only sharpen with a pocketknife: You have gone camping two to three times in your life and bring it up at least once per conversation.

Mechanical pencil: You're taking notes in Algebra 2 class.

MacBook: You like the idea of hiking more than you actually like hiking and are impressed with yourself for liking the Beatles.

Desktop computer: You are either a Serious Writer who needs to be cut off from distraction in order to focus completely on your art, or you are sixty-five years old.

Red pen: You are either grading undergraduate papers, or you are a sociopath.

Micron: Your notebook is the type with the grid dots because you think the lines constrain your creativity but you still need to write straight.

Quill: You have gone to a renaissance faire unironically. Please, for all of our sakes, stop calling women "m'lady."

Tablet: You type with a single finger.

Gel pen: Unless you're writing "HAGS! Don't ever change!" just don't.

Highlighter: . . . Genius, frankly. Break free of the black-or-blue-ink-to-paper paradigm. Redefine art. I salute you.

DON DELILLO

BOLD SIDEBURNS

LONG GRAY HAIR = BADASS

Don DeLillo

(1936–)

MOST INTELLECTUAL

"No sense of the irony of human experience, that we are the highest form of life on earth, and yet ineffably sad because we know what no other animal knows, that we must die."

Who is the writer for our modern and complicated times? If you asked me, perhaps over a glass of rye, I would be forced to say Don DeLillo. Prototypically American—born to a working-class Italian Catholic family in the Bronx—DeLillo captures the ceaseless monotony and misery of our society with a genre he invented out of thin air that's come to be known as "hysterical realism": absurd prose and plot, but hyperdetailed.

Before supporting himself full-time as a novelist, DeLillo had a job in advertising, for Sears Roebuck print ads, among others. Perhaps it's there, in the *Mad Men*–esque annals of capitalism, that he discovered his voice. Although I knew about his work for a long time, most people didn't really pay attention to DeLillo until his National Book Award–winning novel *White Noise*.

It wasn't until the 1970s, in his thirties, that DeLillo began working full-time as a novelist. His first novel, *Americana*, was published in 1971, when DeLillo was thirty-five years old, which is embarrassingly late given I had a short story considered for the *Paris Review* when I was just fifteen. But from then on, he definitely became one of the most prolific and celebrated authors of the era, writing about our crazy, dangerous world and the simulacra of our consumerism-addled media landscape.

DeLILLO WORKS YOU NEED TO KNOW

White Noise [1985]: A professor at a middling, rural university contemplates the meaning of death. His wife, overweight and thus a grotesque clown, is a whore. Our hero calmly plans to murder the dealer his wife slept with in exchange for a drug to make her not fear death. Even the tragic, lonely white male geniuses of our society cannot escape said society.

NOTE

The protagonist of *White Noise* is the head of his university's department of Hitler studies. Take DeLillo's example and feel free to pepper your great novel with Holocaust commentary. If anyone calls it offensive, it's *satire*!

Underworld [1997]: Waste management executive Nick Shay has to deal with issues stemming from an absent father and cheating wife, and he's trying to live in twentieth-century America, if you can imagine.

Cosmopolis (2003): Our hero, Eric Packer, visits his wife of three weeks, a European heiress-slash-poet, and then a prostitute, and goes on to have sex with one of his employees. He loses most of his money by betting incorrectly on the yen. He reflects about his childhood. He has an asymmetrical prostate, which is a big deal (symbolism for how hard it is to be a man).

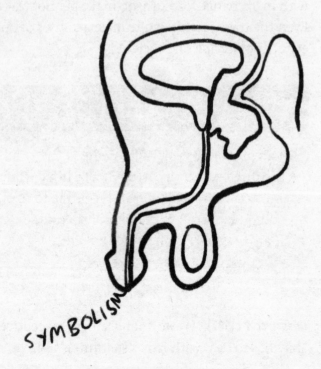

SYMBOLISM

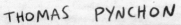

THOMAS PYNCHON

MAYBE BANKSY

PROBABLY WROTE THE NEAPOLITAN NOVELS

SO MYSTERIOUS!!! (SAME.)

ONE DAY I, TOO, WILL BE ON THE SIMPSONS

Thomas Pynchon

[1937–]

MOST LIKELY TO BE A
NO-SHOW AT GRADUATION

*"If they can get you asking the wrong questions,
they don't have to worry about answers."*

Pynchon is notoriously private, and even though he's revealed many details of his life to me via our intimate correspondence, I'll stick to established matters of public record here.

Uncle Pynch was born on Long Island and studied engineering physics at Cornell when he was sixteen years old before dropping out to serve in the navy. After returning to college post-service, Pynchon worked as a technical writer for Boeing in Seattle. He was rejected from a mathematics graduate program at Berkeley, because even they knew that Pynchon's most important work would be done in literature. Only a few photos of Pynchon exist, and he has avoided interactions with reporters for over forty years.

WHAT I'LL LOOK LIKE ON THE SIMPSONS

Like Uncle Pynch, I will also make a voice cameo on *The Simpsons* to prove my cultural dominance.

PYNCHON WORKS YOU NEED TO KNOW

The Crying of Lot 49 [1966]: A woman named Oedipa Maas discovers a long-lost mail-delivering conspiracy, but the novel is really about thermodynamics.

Gravity's Rainbow [1973]: A novel about V-2 rockets developed and launched by the German military at the end of World War II, but it's really about speculative metaphysics.

Inherent Vice [2009]: A comedic detective novel about '70s counterculture—this is the one you should read if the other ones are a little bit too hard for you. I guess someone didn't pay attention in speculative metaphysics class.

Bleeding Edge [2013]: Plot—what is plot anyway? Does it matter? No. The law of the universe is chaos and entropy, which is exactly the point of this book about post–9/11 paranoia and the deep web. The main character, Maxine Tarnow, is a private investigator who also works as a stripper, because you should never write a female protagonist if she's not going to be sexy.

HOW TO DISAPPEAR FOREVER, PART 2

Here is where things become a little trickier. You're going to want to convert all of your assets to cash, and then get all of that cash converted into gold. Use that gold (not cash—cash has markings) to buy an empty lot somewhere between South Dakota and Nebraska. If you find yourself falling in love or getting attached to anyone around you, move away immediately, exactly one state to the west.

On your newly purchased empty lot, the goal is to become a sustenance farmer and exchange as little money (in this case gold) for material goods as possible. A human can live almost entirely on potatoes and milk. Finish building yourself a cabin and cover the roof with turf and grass in order to disguise it as much as possible from satellite imagery. Get your mail delivered to a PO box in a different city. And then, when you're finally alone, write a bestselling cult-classic novel.

RAYMOND CARVER

LEATHER JACKETS
ARE ALWAYS COOL

Raymond Carver

(1938–1988)

MOST LIKELY TO WIN A TONY

"What good are insights? They only make things worse."

Really, the only reason we care about Raymond Carver is because his short stories were expertly edited by Gordon Lish. Some of us don't need editors, Carver. But alas, the Carver-Lish team produced some of our nation's most distinguished short stories and plays, and Carver's is one of the Iowa Writers' Workshop's most distinguished names to drop, even though the truth is he never finished the program.

Carver's performance in academia was always subpar, one imagines because he was always distracted by his own individual literary endeavors. He was only offered a fellowship for his second year of studies at Iowa because his wife personally intervened with the program director and compared her husband's struggles to those of Tennessee Williams. But it didn't matter, because Carver had more important things to work on than finishing his master's. He dropped out, although he *may* have said he had an MFA from Iowa on later CVs. But he was a fiction writer! He was just showing how good he was at writing fiction!

He was eventually admitted to a creative writing program at Stanford and took on a teaching job at the University of California, Berkeley. Other developments in his life: an extramarital affair and a drinking problem. He died at age fifty of lung cancer. Unfortunately, Lish was a surgical editor, but not an actual surgeon.

CARVER WORKS YOU NEED TO KNOW

"Neighbors" (1971): A seemingly happy couple house-sits for their neighbors and revels in the voyeuristic exploration of others' lives. The wife finds photographs she shouldn't have. Can anyone know their neighbors, or even themselves?

"Will You Please Be Quiet, Please?" (1976): Ralph and Marian are two students who fall in love and become teachers. Ralph becomes obsessed with the idea that Marian has been unfaithful to him in the past (probably because all women will break your heart), and when she finally admits that she once cheated, he leaves the house in a rage, plays poker, loses, gets mugged, and then finally returns home, where he discovers that he's magnanimous enough to forgive Marian. The short story was published in 1967's *Best American Short Stories* collection, because it was. The best, I mean.

"What We Talk About When We Talk About Love" (1981): This is the short story they turn into a play in the Oscar-winning film *Birdman*. I don't really watch movies, but I was impressed by the mechanics of the film's illusion of a single continuous shot, which I bet you didn't even realize until now, when I told you.

HOW TO CRITIQUE

Carver was both a student and a faculty member at the prestigious Iowa Writers' Workshop. As a writer in an MFA program (i.e., a real writer), you'll be responsible for evaluating the work of your—for lack of a better word—peers, and administering notes for their improvement. For your edification, I've included a response I wrote to a piece I recently read.

> To *The New Yorker*:
> I think you're off to a decent start here, but several aspects of your piece left me wanting. The epistolary form is interesting, but with only three sentences, I couldn't really discern any legitimate characterization about "The Editors" who wrote the letter.
> I assume in addressing your email to "writer," you were attempting to make a statement on the dehumanizing process of literary rejection, but I found the device pretty obvious and simplistic. Similarly, you say you

"regret" that you were unable to use the material I submitted, a generic verb that fails to convey the emotional turmoil I'm sure you underwent when you determined that my material was too challenging for the reading level of your average subscriber.

Your final sentence (in which you "thank" the writer for the opportunity to read his submission) seems to be falling flat for me— can you use more engaging language here? I personally recommend including a passage from the poem I sent, "Begot by the Pain of Tears and Triumph," to add some much needed nuance to your response.

As it stands, I think your piece has some serious believability issues—as in, I cannot believe anyone would read my poem "Begot by the Pain of Tears and Triumph" and be "unable" to include it in publication. Both your narrative voice and language could use work.

I'll be happy to read any subsequent (significant and very necessary) revisions you may make.

> Yours,
> The author

DAVID FOSTER WALLACE

I'VE READ IT NINE AND A HALF TIMES.

David Foster Wallace

(1962–2008)

VARSITY TENNIS

"The truth will set you free. But not until it is finished with you."

David Foster Wallace was a brilliant, enigmatic genius whose brain was simply too profound for his mortal body to handle. I have a copy of *Infinite Jest* on my person at all times, and I usually bring it to bars to read (or, rather, to reread), waiting for a woman to come up to me so I can immediately begin quizzing her on it.

While growing up, Wallace was a regionally ranked junior tennis player, which is something you could have probably figured out about him if you read *Infinite Jest* like I have. He graduated from Amherst College summa cum laude with a thesis on philosophy and modal logic.

That philosophical mind meant he questioned everything around him. Most people don't realize that David Foster Wallace's parents were liberal, but he voted for Reagan twice. That's the sort of thing I'm thinking about when I tell people that I'm socially liberal but fiscally conservative.

Maybe at one point he had a *minor* romantic obsession with his former partner Mary Karr, whom he regrettably had to throw a coffee table at (a table that he then demanded she pay for). Maybe he tried to push her out of a moving car and while proclaiming his plan to maybe kill her husband (she was married at the time).

And maybe he also kicked her and followed her five-year-old son home from school, climbed up the side of her house, and forced her to change her phone number twice. But that's just the kind of thing a genius *does*. If you read *Infinite Jest*, you would get how amazing he is.

WALLACE WORKS YOU NEED TO KNOW

Infinite Jest [1996]: If you haven't read it, it's pretty hard to describe. I mean, it's postmodern. It's mostly about neocapitalism, and also tennis, and linguistics, and also acronyms.[1]

Consider the Lobster [2005]: Wallace's book of essays includes "Certainly the End of Something or Other, One Would Sort of Have to Think" and "Some Remarks on Kafka's Funniness from Which Probably Not Enough Has Been Removed," both of which were titles that I considered for this book. The title essay was originally published in *Gourmet* magazine and concerns itself with the ethics of boiling lobsters alive in order to make eating them more enjoyable. No one is better at titling essays than DFW. What are we supposed to do? Consider. Consider what? The lobster. It's all there! Truly masterful.

---

1. Also there are a lot of footnotes. And endnotes.

This Is Water (2009): A commencement address delivered to Kenyon College in 2005, *This Is Water* was expanded into a book posthumously four years later. It's less of a speech than a religious text. Use it to define your existence and quote it often. You can also pretend you were there when it was originally delivered, even though obviously you would never attend a place as nondescript as Kenyon.

The Pale King (2011): An unfinished novel published posthumously. May it serve as a reminder: always leave unfinished work to be published after your death. Just imagine how well it will sell.

BRET EASTON ELLIS

I'M GOING TO START MY OWN "LITERARY BRAT PACK"

Bret Easton Ellis

(1964–)

BEST CLIQUE

"*I had all the characteristics of a human being—flesh, blood, skin, hair—but my depersonalization was so intense, had gone so deep, that my normal ability to feel compassion had been eradicated, the victim of a slow, purposeful erasure. I was simply imitating reality, a rough resemblance of a human being, with only a dim corner of my mind functioning.*"

I've mentioned that being a writer now in Los Angeles is an oxymoron. But if anyone is close to achieving the impossible, it's Bret Easton Ellis, although, to be fair, it might be because his most important work takes place in New York City.

Being a writer in Los Angeles is a different experience from being a real writer. If you ever briefly suffer the delusion that you'll work in screenwriting, you'll be shepherded into meetings with executives and posers who wouldn't know quality writing if it bit them on the Pilates-toned ass. You'll have to *drive* places. Most coffee shops offer turmeric lattes. Los Angeles is truly hell. Did I mention the driving? You're trapped in a metal box, bumper to bumper with wannabes and social climbers who only care about being famous. On the subway, you're around *real people*.

But, bless him, Bret Easton Ellis has decided to make a go of it, and for that, I tip my cap.

A literary wunderkind, Easton published his first novel, bestseller *Less Than Zero*, when he was only twenty-one years old.[1] And although he rubbed

---

1. Yes, I am a *few* years older than that now, but when my debut novel finally emerges, you can be sure that it will be a work of considerably more literary sophistication.

shoulders at Bennington College with heavy hitters like Jonathan Lethem (and lesser known and relevant Donna Tartt), it was ultimately with Jay McInerney[2] that Ellis found a similar, kindred spirit with whom to do copious amounts of cocaine.

Four of Ellis's books have made it to the screen, though as a rule they tend to fare better when he's not the one writing the screenplay.

ELLIS WORKS YOU NEED TO KNOW

Less Than Zero [1985]: A satirical black comedy about a student at a private liberal arts college who becomes disillusioned with a lifestyle of partying and by all of his friends, who are drug addicts, sex offenders, and pedophiles. This is very relatable to me, someone who was also once a student at a private liberal arts college who became disillusioned with a lifestyle of partying and by all of my friends.

The Rules of Attraction [1987]: A satirical black comedy about the debauchery of students at a private liberal arts college. Again, just very relatable content here. They made a movie about this, apparently, which I

---

2. Ugh, second person singular? It's just so . . . mundane.

guess Hollywood managed to fit in between predictable superhero blockbusters and remakes.

American Psycho [1991]: A satirical black comedy about the debauchery of Manhattan Wall Street types in the 1980s that makes sure to include murder and also torturing women.

ARE YOU MORE NEW YORK OR LA?

You go to a coffee shop in order to focus on your craft. What do you order?

A. A black coffee.

B. An almond milk matcha.

What is your critically acclaimed debut novel about?

A. A man getting stuck on a subway train and revisiting the weight of all of the mistakes he's made in his twenty-four years of life.

B. A sweeping family drama about migrants crossing the border and the brave white man who meets them and has the guts to tell their story.

What do you eat for breakfast?

A. I don't, because I'm distracted by the hustle and bustle of the world outside me. I'm constantly on the move, engaging with strangers and enemies, friends and lovers.

B. I don't, because gluten before noon muddles the mind and destroys the body. Actually, gluten at any time. Actually, all food.

How explicit are your sex scenes?

A. I describe the curve of her breast.

B. I describe the curve of her [CENSORED BY THE EDITOR FOR PUBLICATION].

What's served at your local cocktail parties?

A. Microbrews and cocaine.

B. Cheese and cocaine.

What are you dressing as for Halloween this year?

A. I don't dress up for Halloween because it's a holiday for children and crass consumerists. So either that or Maxwell Perkins.

B. A serial killer, but one who hasn't been caught yet.

IF YOU ANSWERED MOSTLY A'S

You are a New York writer. Your best work will be done in a notebook while standing on a subway platform, waiting for a train that may or may not ever arrive. The rats that have burrowed beneath your nonfunctional dishwasher are probably just a metaphor for your grandfather's sins.

IF YOU ANSWERED MOSTLY B'S

You are an LA writer. Your best work will be done by dictation while you're waiting in traffic. Your blog posts about the lighting in Tarantino films will one day have upwards of eighty views. Enjoy pretending to call yourself a novelist while you're really just waiting for the right person to read your screenplay.

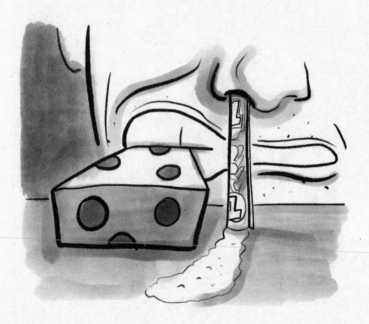

THE JONATHANS

FRANZEN

LETHEM

SAFRAN FOER

AWESOME.

The Jonathans

(1959–)

MOST LIKELY TO LIVE
IN BROOKLYN

"Every good writer I know needs to go into some deep, quiet place to do work that is fully imagined. And what the Internet brings is lots of vulgar data. It is the antithesis of the imagination. It leaves nothing to the imagination."

WHICH JONATHAN...

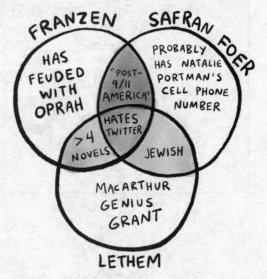

The Jonathans were born in the suburbs of New York City, attended an Ivy League university, and now live in Brooklyn with their wives. Or, rather, they did. Now they live in Brooklyn with their vintage records and the memories of their ex-wives.

They are America's most prominent and prolific White Male Writers, publishing novels every three years and numerous essays for the cover of *The Atlantic* and profiles of other writers for the *New York Times*

Book Review. They are not on social media because there is nothing more frivolous than the brain-rotting drivel of the masses, the impulse to trivialize every thought by squeezing it into 140 characters and sending it out into the grasping, impatient childlike fists of the world. Thoughts should be written down in Moleskine journals, contemplated for three weeks, and then developed into a 4,000-word essay for *The New Yorker.* Maybe an essay on the nature of essays?

The Jonathans drink at a kitschy Red Hook dive bar and order their drinks neat. They get weekly drinks with Don DeLillo, but they only mention that the second time you have a conversation with them because they don't care about all of that name-dropping, celebrity-lifestyle bullshit. Instead, they care about, in decreasing order of importance: the state of literature, the Jewish diaspora, 9/11, hard-wood furniture, and birds.

JONATHANS WORKS YOU NEED TO KNOW

The one about a detective: But the main character is really Brooklyn.

The one about post–9/11 America: How has 9/11 changed the psyche of our nation? *Has* 9/11 changed the psyche of our nation? The answer, as it turns out, is yes.

The other one about post–9/11 America: This one talks way more about 9/11.

That novel that's actually about birds: You didn't want to talk about birds, did you? Because I would love to talk about some birds.

HOW TO IDENTIFY CHICK LIT

There is nothing more corrosive to the state of the world right now than women writing books for other women to enjoy. Identify chick lit using the following criteria, and sneer at it on sight:

- A cover featuring a woman from behind, with her hair down. This woman is probably standing on a beach, or near a field, or in an office. If you can see her feet, she is either wearing six-inch heels, or she is barefoot.

- "Girl" and/or "Daughter" and/or "Wife" in the title.

- A plot involving someone trying to get a promotion at work. The main character probably works too hard and thinks everything in her life will come together as soon as she has a promotion when everything is derailed by some big misunderstanding or kerfuffle that sets her entire life awry.

- A female protagonist.

- An Oprah's Book Club sticker. No matter what book it's on, that sticker means the book is able to be read and understood by suburban middle-American women, which means it's not real literature. Truly, no one has done more to damage the American literary community than Oprah, who insists that books are for the masses. Unless the sticker is on *your* book, in which case you can humbly accept the honor (and the increase in sales) while still rolling your eyes about it.

- "By Jennifer Weiner."

AFTERWORD

Well, there you have it. Everything you need to know in order to swirl your cognac with confidence at your MFA program's upcoming mixer. A few final pieces of advice:

1. Never assume a woman has ever read anything in her entire life. Just explain it to her. It'll save her the embarrassment of having to ask.

2. Nothing you write is ever bad. If someone thinks it's bad, she just doesn't understand it.

3. Writing is a full-time job, and doing anything else to make "money" is failure. I mean, it's lazy! Why would you give up and start doing something else? Worst-case scenario, just dip into your trust fund.

4. If you don't know how to critique a piece someone else has written, repeat after me: "The ending just didn't feel *earned*."

5. If you have a social media account, make sure you spend most of your time there reminding other people how inane social media is.

6. Women will never understand you.

7. If anyone ever tells you that he or she read the

Fifty Shades of Grey books and enjoyed them, you are duty-bound to kill him or her on sight.

8. A mattress on the floor makes perfect sense for you. You are so focused on your craft, you can't even be bothered to find a headboard. Headboards are for nonwriters.

9. Write drunk, edit never.

10. You are a White Man, goddammit, and don't you ever forget it.

THE WHITE MAN'S GUIDE TO WHITE MALE WRITERS OF THE WESTERN CANON READING LIST

Martin Amis, *The Rachel Papers*

Christopher Buckley, *Thank You for Smoking*

Charles Bukowski, *Ham on Rye* and *Women*

William S. Burroughs, *Naked Lunch*

Albert Camus, *The Outsider*

Raymond Carver, *Where I'm Calling From*

Michael Chabon, *The Amazing Adventures of Kavalier & Clay*

John Cheever, *Falconer*

Joshua Cohen, *Book of Numbers*

Joseph Conrad, *Heart of Darkness*

Don DeLillo, *Underworld* and *White Noise*

Charles Dickens, *David Copperfield*

Fyodor Dostoevsky, *Crime and Punishment*

Umberto Eco, *Foucault's Pendulum*

Dave Eggers, *A Heartbreaking Work of Staggering Genius*

Bret Easton Ellis, *American Psycho*

William Faulkner, *As I Lay Dying*

Jonathan Franzen, *The Kraus Project*

William Golding, *Lord of the Flies*
Ernest Hemingway, *A Farewell to Arms* and *The Sun Also Rises*
Homer, *The Odyssey*
John Irving, *A Widow for One Year*
James Joyce, *Ulysses*
Franz Kafka, *Metamorphosis*
Jack Kerouac, *On the Road*
John Knowles, *A Separate Peace*
Jonathan Lethem, *Motherless Brooklyn*
Karl Marx, *The Communist Manifesto*
Cormac McCarthy, *Blood Meridian, The Crossing,* and *The Road*
Ian McEwan, *The Cement Garden*
Jay McInerney, *Bright Lights, Big City*
Herman Melville, *Moby-Dick*
John Milton, *Paradise Lost*
Alan Moore, *Watchmen*
Vladimir Nabokov, *Lolita* and *Pale Fire*
Tim O'Brien, *The Things They Carried*
George Orwell, *1984*
Marcel Proust, *À la recherche du temps perdu*
Thomas Pynchon, *Gravity's Rainbow*
Tom Robbins, *Even Cowgirls Get the Blues*
J. D. Salinger, *The Catcher in the Rye*
William Shakespeare, *Hamlet* and *Macbeth*
John Steinbeck, *East of Eden*

Henry David Thoreau, *Walden*
Leo Tolstoy, *Anna Karenina* and *War and Peace*
Virgil, *The Aeneid*
Kurt Vonnegut, *Slaughterhouse-Five*
David Foster Wallace, *Infinite Jest*
Evelyn Waugh,[1] *Brideshead Revisited*

---

1. Don't worry, he's actually a man.

ACKNOWLEDGMENTS

I would like to thank the glass of whiskey I kept as my constant companion while writing, the typewriter with its cheerful, maddening clacks, my loyal fountain pen, and, of course, the memory of David Foster Wallace.

To Sarah Haugen at Harper Perennial for having the guts to finally put my work into the world, and to my agent, Dan Mandel, for seeing the brilliance in the coffee-stained sheets of notebook paper that I mailed unsolicited to your office.

Jason, my endless appreciation for your little drawings. *The New Yorker* has gone a bit downhill, but still I find your work charming. And though I personally don't engage with "comics," nor do I typically engage with books with pictures, I understand that sometimes the masses need a bit of spoon-feeding.

ABOUT THE AUTHOR
AND ILLUSTRATOR

Dana Schwartz (@DanaSchwartzzz) is an arts and culture writer whose work has appeared in *Entertainment Weekly, Marie Claire, GQ, Bustle, Glamour, Vanity Fair*, NewYorker.com, the *Guardian*, Mental_Floss, VICE, *Brooklyn Magazine*, and more. She's the creator of popular literary Twitter accounts @GuyInYourMFA and @DystopianYA, and the author of the memoir *Choose Your Own Disaster*, and the young-adult novel *And We're Off*. Dana lives in Los Angeles with her cat, Beetlejuice.

Jason Adam Katzenstein is a cartoonist and writer for print and television. His work has appeared in *The New Yorker*, the *New York Times* and *MAD Magazine*, and on Cartoon Network. Jason is the illustrator of the graphic novel *Camp Midnight* for Image Comics, written by Steven T. Seagle. He is a visiting professor at Wesleyan University.